Collecting Conversations

In memory of Mum

For my Bunch:
Martin, Connie, Anna & James

Sam Bunch

P

First published
Parks Publications, London
in 2018

Sam Bunch © 2017

A CIP catalogue record for this book
is available from the British Library.

ISBN 978-1-9998804-0-8

2nd printrun 2018
Printed and bound in China

Design **Alison Gardner**
Illustrations **Charlotte Hardy**
Editor **Su O'Brien**
Proof reader **Sian Morrissey**

Follow me at:
collectingconversations.com

Contents

PART ONE –

WHY I WROTE THIS BOOK

PART TWO – THE QUESTIONS

Foreward

There is a fear that we live in a 'swipe' culture. We've all seen it: eyes down, earphones in, thumbs swiping through multiple shiny glittering options. A famous academic Zgymunt Bauman worried about what this 'swipe' culture was doing to us. "Where is the humanity" he asked, "when we can 'friend' or 'defriend' in a single swipe? Where is the richness of a relationship that is developed and worked at?" Speaking from a marriage of 61 years, we can guess that he knew what he was talking about. Bauman was worried that we had lost the ability to connect and, having witnessed the holocaust, he perhaps had greater insight into the horrors that follow from disconnection: when we stop connecting we stop caring for each other. We experience this disconnection in our everyday lives when we lose the skills to talk and to listen to each other. That we can feel lonely, fearful, anxious or just bewildered when we lose these skills, is all down to the fact that we are fundamentally social creatures. In the recent best seller 'Sapiens: A Brief History of Humankind', the author Yuval Noah Harari claims that it's our ability to tell stories that makes us human. Stories require connections – not just a teller and listener but connections of lives and imaginations: stories draw us together and enrich our lives.

We all know the big stories that make up history – those stories of empires and dynasties – but there's been more interest of late in everyday stories of everyday and ordinary folk. We are drawn to these because this is where life is: the crushing sadness of grief, breath-taking highs of love, the constant drip of worry, the lightness and weight of companionship, and the daily stuff of just getting on with things. Of course we do more than tell our stories, in their telling we are emboldened to change, to accept, to forgive or we might find some momentary peace in the sharing of our lives and the connection stories bring. And of course we learn from listening – how else can those of us who have never experienced getting old or feeling grief learn about how these may feel?

Zgymunt would have approved of how Sam and I met. It was on a packed Virgin train from London to Liverpool. I plonked down at one of those all-too-small tables and sprung open my laptop. Next to me was a woman also juggling laptop, phone and coffee cup. As we did that very English thing of apologizing

and throwing up our eyebrows at the ridiculous situation Virgin placed us in, we soon fell into sharing our stories. Of course stories start quite mildly. We started by sharing what we were each working on. I was working on a project that involved collecting positive experiences of women getting older and Sam, well, she was working on this wonderful book. Our projects were so similar and yet so different that we shut those laptops and fell into a conversation that ranged from our recent losses, love, childhood, bodies, work, the North, and our future: we shared our lives and laughed through most of it. I'm not sure what the rest of the train carriage thought but it was the start of an on-going friendship that led me to reading this book you hold in your hands now.

This is a book of stories but it's also a book about stories. It's a book of people's lives – particularly women's lives. This is important because women's stories are often dismissed as gossip or tittle tattle: the expression 'old wives tales' does not refer to accumulated wisdom but something childish, ill-informed and laughable. There is no coincidence that women also feel excluded or invisible as they get older: we have to reclaim our voices and our lives. This book shows we have more to offer and we have much to learn from each other.

Much of what you will read are understated single sentence comments but they are raindrops that contain entire universes. These sentences open those everyday worlds of emotion and struggle – worlds that are familiar and alien to us and worlds we might be frightened of. These short sentences are how stories work – we are invited to fill in the gaps, flesh things out with our imagination, to reflect on our own lives: we are transported into life itself by what may look like a mundane comment. Such is the power of stories.

Sam's book then, contains worlds of experience and worlds of connections. It will make you grimace with recognition, smile and reflect – but most of all it will encourage us all to say 'Hi, how are you?' and make new connections and help make life more human again.

Jayne Raisborough
Professor of Media and Culture, Leeds Beckett University, Leeds, August 2017

Self doubt alert...

This project has shown me that self doubt is rife! Most of the women I spoke to hadn't escaped its claws. Now that I know it's a 'normal' and an ordinary sensation why does it still feel extraordinarily uncomfortable?

Up until this point in my life I've not written much more than an email. Talking about writing a book (or talking about anything for that matter) and doing it are two very different things. An unfamiliar inner voice emerged; 'I can't, I don't know how to and why would anyone want to read what I've got to say?' became my daily mantra. I now became riddled with self doubt.

During the writing period of this book I felt exposed and vulnerable. Very slowly I've learned to adapt and accept these feelings. They haven't gone away and at times are still excruciating. Does it matter? Not really. It's only my ego telling me I'm not good enough and if I'd let that voice stop me, I wouldn't be sharing this beautiful book with you now.

'Collecting Conversations' isn't an ordinary book but it is about ordinary things. It's a very honest book. It grapples with life. It tells us what's going on in our daily realities and shows us that we all need to look after our everyday. After all, it's what we do every day that matters.

My hope is that when you've finished reading this you'll feel inspired and comfortable enough to give something new a go yourself. I bet there are projects you've never started? An itch dying to be scratched? What's stopping you? Very likely, self doubt! But, if you don't give it a go, you'll kick yourself.

It doesn't matter however big or small the idea, whatever it is, give it a go. Get uncomfortable. Learn something new. Anyone can write, draw, cook, fill in the gap… if you want to.

As we age, our confidence often plummets. Have fun and play; it's often when you're not thinking that things start to take shape. Explosions of creativity boost confidence. If we change the way we think about ourselves, others will too. Please don't put limits on yourself.

Here's my offering:

Introduction

My breakfast ritual of gutting the juicy inners from grapefruits got me thinking; how did I ever learn to do this? As with most mundane tasks, it was my Mum who taught me. Since she died I find myself making these observations. Equally it could be whilst I'm mashing the spuds or peeling carrots. It's those simple, everyday tasks that trigger something in me and, if I let it, makes me feel sad.

I've now started to wonder about the future tasks. How on earth do you raise teenagers. Should I dye my hair when it starts to go grey? And what about this menopause I keep hearing about? There were certainly going to be more questions. Who's going to be at the end of the phone when I have a crisis of confidence now?

Thankfully Mum left diaries. I'd found them at the back of her wardrobe. For 30 years she had written one liners about everyday life. Her diaries made me wonder about how other women 'do life'. What if I spoke to some women and asked them, would I find my answers there?

Using the subjects Mum mentions in her diaries, I came up with a list of questions and in between the school run, I began interviewing women at my kitchen table. Asking questions from the deep and meaningful to the seemingly mundane. I gathered 107 women in total. I listened to their words and advice. I learned that all you have to do is ask and the knowledge, wisdom and inspiration comes rolling in.

After listening to hundreds of hours worth of life experiences, I was inspired to share what I'd heard. This is when I squeezed out of my comfort zone and tried something new – writing! It was awkward and many times I wanted to stop but years later, and after many cringeworthy moments, I have the pleasure in sharing this wonderful book.

It's a book in two parts:
The first part is my story; from the impact Mum dying had on me, to how you've ended up with this book in your hands. The second part is the commentary of conversations I had with the 107 women I interviewed. In bite-size pieces they reveal their innermost thoughts through some honest and open conversations. With their permission, you're getting a little dose of what most of us think and feel at some point in our lives. It's a warm blanket of generous spirit from these wise and wonderful women.

Part One

Why I wrote this book

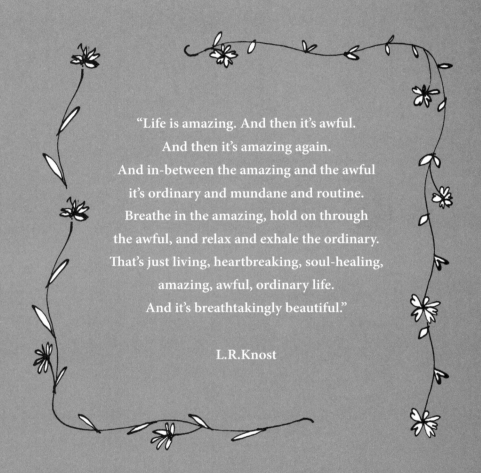

"Life is amazing. And then it's awful.
And then it's amazing again.
And in-between the amazing and the awful
it's ordinary and mundane and routine.
Breathe in the amazing, hold on through
the awful, and relax and exhale the ordinary.
That's just living, heartbreaking, soul-healing,
amazing, awful, ordinary life.
And it's breathtakingly beautiful."

L.R.Knost

Winter

December 26th. It's cold, the snow hasn't quite settled – it hardly ever does in London. We're sat at the kitchen table, immediate family and friends, eating and drinking our body weight in leftovers. Well, it is Christmas. The phone goes, it's 8pm and it's my brother. It's not an unexpected call but I can hear the urgency in his voice: he tells me to come now, there's not long left.

I've been drinking, so I can't drive and, after a quick Google search, find that there are no trains up the west coast over the festive period thanks to engineering works. I'll have to go up the east coast via Leeds first thing in the morning.

Our guests abruptly leave and we clear up the mess. I'm in a panic. I need to be there, but I can't get there. I've never wanted time to pass more quickly. Bedtime comes and I try and sleep. I can't. It's all very real and seemingly it's come a bit too quick. We knew Mum didn't have long, but we thought another six months at least.

I toss and turn 'til 4am, by which time I think I may as well get up. I run a bath and soak in the remnants of the night's moon still shining through the window, and wonder what the day will bring. I quickly dress and head out into the cold morning air, my teeth chattering as I hot-foot it to Clapham Common tube station. It's uncharacteristically quiet. However, 20 minutes later when I arrive at Kings Cross, it's business as usual: busy, busy, busy. Is London ever quiet for long?

I'm early. I collect my ticket and look around the station for a seat: all taken. Then, strangely, a man offers me his. I thank him. As I open my book and start to read, another man comes up to me and says, 'God bless you'. These are unusual happenings, especially in London, and now I'm sure it's going be a day like no other.

The 7am to Leeds is ready to leave. I board and settle in for the journey. Quite quickly, I start to feel sick. Is it the motion of the train or the unnerving reality

that this will be my last visit to see my Mum? I open my book and as I turn the page, I read, 'That morning, Pat died'. My Mum's name is Pat!

My tummy is in knots. I need the loo. But there's no way I'm going on the train. The memory of my sister's awkward moment when she forgot to press 'lock' on one of those wrap around loos they have on Virgin trains. There she was, knickers round her ankles, for all the world to see and an image hard to erase from my mind.

Two hours later we pull into Leeds – I'm desperate. There's no time to go, or I'll miss my connection. I dash over to the next platform, jump on the train and we set off. Just two stops to Shipley that's all. Can I hold on? I can think of nothing else. Talk about distraction! I step off the train and typically it's pouring down. My brother is there to meet me.

'Can't stop, need the loo!'. I rush straight past him through the torrential rain across the station car park into McDonald's loo: the relief. My world fell out of me right there and then! Too much information? Most definitely but if I am to tell my tale then you need to hear everything. I was in pain and I needed to let go. I'd decided my desperation was a metaphor for what was happening. Now I had let go I was ready to face what was to come.

Somewhere, in my deepest recesses, I'd feared this day since I was a child. I'd always worried about Mum dying. I'm not sure if the impact of her and Dad splitting up when I was little had made me paranoid. For a few years she'd been our only parent, and I was petrified she'd die and then what would happen to us?

It's still early as my brother and I set off over the moors. It's windy, misty and the rain doesn't let up. His clapped-out car is in a state, the windows don't close properly and the wipers do a poor job at cutting though the horizontal downpour. Some days you can actually see the picturesque landscapes over the moors, but not today: it's miserable.

The hour-long journey across the hills is all very symbolic. Never mind 'Jerusalem' with its 'pleasant pastures seen' – we can't see a thing. It is wet and grim. We banter our way through the first half of the journey then settle in to the Carpenters Greatest Hits, singing full pelt to 'Rainy Days And Mondays'.

At last, we arrive in the vicinity of home. There's a sense of familiarity that grounds me. Every time I come back to my village there's a feeling of

homecoming. I'm connected there; I don't know why. I've lived in London way longer than I ever lived in Lancashire, but my roots are strong.

From the moors, we head towards Read; via Fence, Higham and Simonstone, skirting the base of Pendle Hill (home to the infamous Lancashire Witches). Apart from the modern bypass, all the villages have a feeling of a bygone era. Sleepy, weathered farmhouses and rural farmland landscapes that have hardly changed in decades. Beautiful dry stone walls divide fields and fields of undulating landscapes. These walls are furred with succulent green moss. It's one of nature's delights – and mine too. I have been known to spend quite a bit of time gazing into the tiniest worlds that inhabit these walls. Watching the smallest dewdrop balancing on the lichen can transport me into a whole other world. There's comfort for me in that this scene would have been familiar to my ancestors who have lived around this area since the early 16th Century, if not longer.

We weave along windy roads for a mile or so, before coming to a crossroads. This landmark takes me back to my childhood. On the corner there used to be a shop once owned by a man called Eddie. Back in the Seventies, when we were kids and there wasn't much happening, we'd venture up to Eddie's to buy bags of boiled sweets weighed out from the many jars he had lining the shelves. We'd spend the rest of the day idly wandering around the country lanes, sidetracking up farm tracks, sitting on styles and occasionally fishing for perch. It was all very Enid Blyton. I remember Mum telling us that when she was a teenager, she and her crowd would wander up to Eddie's too. Back then, you could sit in at the counter on a bar stool and drink banana milkshakes. It was Read's very own Ed's Easy Diner!

The road from Eddie's to ours is a narrow country lane we call 'The Tops'. It is decorated with different styles of houses ranging from traditional farmhouses, large detached houses and quaint cottages. It's very pretty. A little while later we come onto Straits Lane, where there are a couple of 1970s housing estates and more traditional terraces on one side, and an idyllic English village setting on the other: a church, lush green fields, sheep, horses and cows often found sheltering under the trees from the never-ending rain.

Historically, Read housed two cotton mills, a cobbler that supplied the mill workers with clogs, and a few shops, one of which – the village newsagents – was eventually owned by my Mum and my new Stepdad, John (who I now call

Dad). As kids, my sister and I were always on standby to do the paper rounds if the regulars didn't turn up, which was more often than not. Consequently, we knew every letter box, the name of every house, road and street. It's not really a village anymore. Its population combined with adjoining village Simonstone is about 2,500.

Mum was brought up here. She went to the local school, as did I. Growing up in a village, especially when your Mum and Dad run the local shop, has its advantages; you get to know everyone and everything from the 'pop' man (delivering fizzy drinks by van), the coal man and the rag and bone man to all the old ladies in their housecoats, curlers and plastic rain hats. It was a different era, and, although it was the Seventies, in many ways it felt a bit like the Fifties.

We turn into our road and pull into the drive with a sinking feeling. A deep breath, and this is it: the beginning of the end.

Dad's sitting at the kitchen table, head in his newspaper and a usual fag in hand. He's looking distracted. He's not really doing the Sudoku. He's avoiding what's happening upstairs. A quick peck on his cheek. I say 'Hi', and dash upstairs where I'm greeted by an unfamiliar scene.

Three women were sat in vigil around Mum's bed. What had happened? I'd only seen her ten days before, and she was fine. I know she wasn't well, but she wasn't at death's door: now she was. There was no changing this storyline, she was going to die and it was going to be soon. She was asleep but restless. Her face stretched tight. She was hot, swollen and breathing very loudly – and I mean deafening. Mum's best friends were chatting away. They all looked fairly relaxed under the circumstances. Christine, Mum's neighbour, tells me the noise is the death rattle. It's awful. Too loud and it grates. It seems so out of character with what's happening. Shouldn't this scene be very quiet, serene and calm? Shouldn't it?

I've never seen anyone die before, although I had seen a dead body years ago. I'm a complementary therapist and, when an old Jamaican client of mine died, I was invited to the funeral in Brixton, South London. I'd never been to a funeral like it. It was heaving with hundreds of people, all from Caribbean descent. I felt a little out of place. I was literally the only white person there.

Everybody went up to the open casket to pay their respects. I wasn't sure I

wanted to but it would have been more awkward if I hadn't, so I got in line. She looked weird. She looked like she'd come straight off a scene in 'Little House On The Prairie'. She wore a long white night gown and had a bonnet on, a proper mop cap, really old-fashioned, and her skin was all waxy. I didn't like it. I moved quickly along.

Mum isn't waxy; well not yet. Thankfully she's not in pain as she's morphined up to the hilt. Every now and then there's a 'click' from the machine she's attached to, dripping in the poison that's slowly taking her away.

I'm overcome with sadness and, in a moment of desperation, I lean over her and firmly tell her to go.

'Go Mum, go! It's time, please just go!'.

I want her to die. I want her to leave her body and be at peace. Everyone says when someone dies, 'They're at peace now'. I never really took it so literally, but now I do. I want her to go, she looks tired. I take the glass of water from the bedside table and put my arm under her head to try and get some fluid into her. There's no point, she can't swallow and I'm making matters worse. It's going straight into her lungs and now she's choking.

Christine assures me everything is okay and we just have to sit and wait. These women have been sat here for hours holding vigil and I've waltzed in upsetting the apple cart. I take my place around the bedside and we talk – not quietly, mind, it's too noisy. We chat and catch up on gossip. It all seems surreal but at the same time comforting, caring and, strangely normal.

A few hours pass. One by one, Mum's friends get up to leave. They kiss Mum and say their final goodbyes. It's now just me and Mum. My brother and Dad are downstairs. My sister Sally was in America visiting her husband when she got the Boxing Day phone call and is now on a plane. I'm not sure she'll make it back in time.

There are two single beds in Mum's room; the double has been replaced by an old single and one of those nasty, plasticky hospital beds. Dad's put himself in the spare room. He's not coping too well. I get ready for bed and wonder what the night will bring.

I'm in bed with the duvet wrapped tightly around my body, making sure there are no air pockets. I resemble a Mummy. It's bloody freezing. I can see my

breath. For a moment I wonder if I should talk or not. It's not as though she'll hear me with that racket going on. Nevertheless I start chatting just like we used to but, this time, it was going to be a one-way conversation. I tell her about my kids and what's been going on back home in London. I tell her that Sally is on a flight and trying to get here. I pause for a moment then tell her, 'I'm a bit scared. What am I going to do if you die when I'm asleep? What do I do if I wake up and you're gone?' I am now not a 40-year-old woman, I'm a four-year-old child. I need my mum to tell me what to do. I've never done this before and I'm worried I might do it wrong. Hours later, I drift off.

I wake to hear silence. I turn over and see that Mum has shrunk, she's tiny. The rattle has stopped and she's now still and silent. I lean over, she's not dead but not far off. She's cold.

Christine didn't go home. Whilst I was sleeping she was checking on Mum throughout the night, up and down the stairs busying herself washing up and making tea for the men folk. She peers her head round the bedroom door and I beckon her in. She offers to make a brew. You can't beat a nice cup of tea when the going gets tough. As she leaves, my brother comes in. I open the curtains to once again greet the rain and a new day begins. My sister is busting a gut to get here.

I sit with my brother on the window sill. I look over at Mum. There's something foaming from her mouth. As I get a tissue to wipe her lips I realise she'd just taken her last breath.

The reality of watching someone die is quite shocking. It's very final: they are no more. Up until that point even though you know they're going to die, they're still alive. They still have blood running through their veins but the minute that stops it all changes and it's not very nice.

Within minutes there's a sound at the window I turn to look. It's blowing a gale. There must be 50 birds – blue tits, I think – hovering at the window. They don't stay long, but long enough for me to realise it's another sign. They're taking her spirit away. My brother, however, isn't convinced!

Christine comes back in with a cup of tea and a white carrier bag. I tell her Mum's dead. 'I knew it' she says, 'I had a feeling she didn't want me in the room

when it was time although I did feel her spirit go about 5 this morning'.

I feared something strange was about to happen. Christine pulls a bandage and a white sheet out of the bag. She ties the bandage around Mum's head. I'm having flashbacks to the 'Little House On The Prairie' again. What is it with the whole bonnet look? Sure enough my Mum looks ridiculous. Christine senses my distaste and says, 'Her mouth will stay open if we don't hold it shut until after rigor mortis has set in'. She's knows what she's talking about, she's done this many times before but I'm still not convinced.

The waxy pallor comes on quickly. It turns my stomach, and for some reason I feel a bit scared again. I distract myself by 'freshening' Mum up. I spray her with a bit of perfume and apply her favourite lipstick to try and perk her up a bit. Now she does looks ridiculous.

My sister eventually arrives, having broken speed limits getting from the airport, but misses Mum by ten minutes. We leave them alone for a while. And then the cleaning starts.

Apparently it's quite normal to start cleaning after someone has died. A 'natural instinct', I'm told! Women appear from nowhere and there's a flurry of activity. The house wasn't even messy in the first place. Gez, a family friend, arrives with her Marigolds and starts attacking the bathroom. Christine moves furniture around and I start hoovering. Someone is even cleaning the windows. Everything is tidied, moved and hoovered. Well, all except Mum – she's lying there like Snow White, devoid of all clinical attire and covered in a pristine, starched white sheet. Another thing I don't understand.

The doctor has to come round to make sure she's dead. He confirms what we already know. She's dead! A little while later the undertaker comes. As quick as a flash in a no – nonsense manner he slips her into a body bag and putting her over his shoulder like a sack of coal, carries her away. Nothing ceremonious, just practical and matter-of-fact.

So, that was that. Mum was dead and the house was clean. Now what? Well, my Dad, for one, doesn't like to hang around. We sped off to Burnley town hall to register the death. If it hadn't been Christmas I think she'd have been buried that night.

The next day my sister wanted to go and see Mum 'resting'. I didn't. But with her excellent persuasive powers, she drags me off to Bertwistle's funeral parlour

down Riley Street in Padiham. She shoves a photo of Mum in my hand and says 'Give it to the funeral director and tell him to make her look nice'. I did as I was told, only to be humorously rebuffed. In a thick northern accent, Mr Bertwistle says 'Look, love, we're not flipping hairdressers. She'll be reet, not as though she's going nowhere'. We laughed; the ice was broken. We instantly felt comforted.

We went in to see Mum. There she was, her tiny body lying in her coffin. The room was cold as ice. Goodness knows what we were thinking, but we were laden with talismans and gifts – things we thought she'd like! We lay them around her body. It was our own Egyptian funerary ritual. There were cards, chocolate, photographs. I'd put in a clay toadstool that I'd made when I was a kid in art class. She'd had it in her wardrobe all these years. I assumed if she'd kept it that long, then it should rightfully go with her onto the next life.

Mum had written her own funeral; she wanted to be buried with her mum and dad. There was one space left in the family burial plot that she'd 'bagsied' years ago. She'd requested Frank Sinatra 'My Way' going up the aisle and Doris Day 'Que Sera Sera' coming back down. I admired her foresight. It was much easier organising her funeral knowing what she wanted.

In the churchyard, the weather once again greets us with intrusive brutality. Horizontal ice cold rain and gales. If it wasn't so sad it would have been hilarious. Her coffin is lowered six feet into the ground only to be jetted back about three feet by the water. It's now a burial at sea! In that moment I make a decision. I'm opting for a cremation and my ashes scattered over Pendle Hill, please.

No one hangs around for longer than necessary. The cold wind makes it unbearable. After the burial, we congregate at the 'Simmy', a local hotel, for meat and potato pie and chicken butties. It's a grim affair. It's definitely not a celebration of her life. Dad shuts himself away in the back room, and we muddle our way through it.

Later that evening, very tired, sad and a little numb, me and my family travel back home to London where, to finish off an awful day, we have a puncture on the M40! I start to laugh and feel strangely comforted by yet another sign: Mum never did like us leaving. She would feel flat for days and wished we all lived nearer.

New Year

I'm slowly becoming stuck. My world has gone inwards and it isn't looking good. 'Maudlin', I think, is the term. The monotony of daily life coupled with grief is all becoming a bit much. The everyday routine of cooking and taxiing children about is hardly fulfilling. Heightened by my sadness, something needed to happen or, over time, I can see my mood and the monotony turning into over-eating, over-thinking, and me heading towards a mental crisis.

Having never done grief before, I'm not sure what's going to happen. Not much has happened since the funeral three weeks earlier. Friends tell me to be kind to myself, not to take on too much, to rest and eat properly. Well that's not going to happen: I've three children to look after and cake is my best friend.

Domesticity and the daily routine never lets up and I'm desperate for some space. I just want to be alone. I'm turning into Greta bloody Garbo. My husband is irritating me too. There's something about death that shakes you up. Everything in your life that's not quite right seems to grab your attention in full disco lights.

Things are changing, everything is becoming unsettled. Last autumn we'd booked a skiing holiday for half term, and now I really wish we hadn't. We're not a skiing family; the kids have never been before. Right now the idea sounds all a bit much. The night before, as I'm trying to pack, my four-year-old is playing up. From nowhere, I burst into tears. It's not like me. It's not about whether I should or shouldn't cry, normally I just don't. So it comes as a bit of a shock when my mouth opens and out comes a sort of guttural 'I miss my Mum'. I'm fragile and this is a new sensation.

Bright and not so breezy, the next morning we head to the Alps and start a week of hard work. What should have been a lovely, energising holiday amongst snow-covered mountains, surrounded by pine trees and fresh air, turns out to be one long arduous affair. Skiing is hard enough when you just have yourself to think about, but carrying clobber for three kids and the agony of trying to

walk in painful, rigid boots was all a bit much, as was going back and forth to the chalet for more stuff, less stuff and endless toilet runs. I'm glad to get home.

Time waits for nobody and the daily routine picks up speed again. My husband and I have tickets to see The Eagles at the O2. I spend most of the evening watching a mum and her daughter in the row in front singing and dancing together. I'm feeling sad but who am I kidding? I would never have done that with my Mum. We just weren't like that. So now I'm overdosing on nostalgia and grieving something that I never had. I really am indulging myself.

Meanwhile, my Dad is not doing so well either. In fact he's been going on dating sites – already! He's in danger of becoming a stereotype. I'll have to step in quickly, or I might end up with a new mum the same age as me – or younger!

I nominate myself 'Matchmaker'. Luck was on my side. At a friend's party I get chatting to her mum. She's lovely. Instantly I ask her if she fancies going on a date with my Dad. Not my usual greeting, admittedly, but from where I was sitting my Dad's situation was desperate. Surprisingly, she says yes! Bingo! How can it fail? I'm a natural. A couple of weeks later, I set them up and they go out on a date.

I think getting older must be fun. You don't have to play games and pussyfoot around anymore. You can just say it like it is and they said it… they liked each other and I am clearly heading towards a new career path.

Normality and routine continue, but something weird is happening. A fly enters my life. Bear with me, I know how this sounds…

I have a room in the attic where I meditate. I pop in there most days for a bit of peace. So there I was, a few months after Mum died, sitting quietly, wrapped in a blanket getting all snuggly. I light my oil burner and, with the fragrant smell of geranium wafting over me, I sink into meditation. Almost immediately I can hear a fly. It has come in through the open window. Flies often come in, quickly realise their mistake and spend the rest of their time bashing their heads against the window trying to get out, but not this one. Even with my eyes shut, I can sense it. It isn't buzzing around and it is quite still. I have a quick peep. It's just sitting on the arm of my chair. Twenty minutes later, it is still there.

I don't think anything more about it but, a few days later, the same thing happens again. This time I decide it is a sign. My Mum has come back as a fly. I go downstairs to tell my kids what happened. They humour me.

Similar scenarios happen enough times over the next few years for me to appreciate that it's a bit odd. It becomes a bit of a story. 'Your gran's back', I tell the kids. They tell their friends and I start to get a bit of a reputation for being the woman who thinks her dead mother has come back as a fly.

There's more on the fly later. It gets better…promise! Oh and just for ease, I shall now address my fly as 'she'.

Life carries on, with the school run, shopping, tidying, cooking, homework and the kids' after-school clubs. I've volunteered myself to help run the swimming club where my eldest, Connie, is one of the three hundred swimmers. It is turning out to be a full-time job and not much fun either. I seem to have dived straight in at the deep end into an inhospitable bunch of overly-competitive parents. I'm not sure I have the stomach for this.

By stark contrast, I have started helping at the local hospice in Clapham. It is only a morning a week but I like it. In fact, I remember texting a friend to say, 'Should I be enjoying this as much as I am?' I only sit with the patients. Sometimes we chat, other times I just listen.

Then – there was Paul, a young, homeless man. This particular morning he calls me over. He shows me his legs – they were weeping. He wasn't in pain but fluid was coming out of all the pores in his legs, like he was bursting. All the nursing staff were busy so I asked him if he would like me to wash his legs. There was something in doing something so simple and being in that moment with him that was a huge privilege. He died just a few days later. I'm glad I had my moment with him. It felt very healing.

It is almost two years now since Mum died. They say it takes two years to get through the grief, well, I'm not sure who 'they' are, but they seem to be right. Just six weeks before the two-year anniversary, I feel something shift. It's a strange feeling because I didn't know I'd been under a veil until it lifted. Suddenly I feel more like me again, although freer and somehow liberated. I was inspired by life again and I was back with a new-found sense of freedom.

All is well with the world. My Dad is having a great time. He's got engaged and he's happy. He's flown across the Atlantic for the first time in his life and, the icing on the cake, he bought himself a Jag! He had always wanted one. His dream, ever since I could remember, was to own a maroon XJS, like the one Simon Templar drove in the 1970s TV series 'The Saint'. So, when he turned up at my house grinning like a Cheshire Cat, I was quite surprised to see he'd got himself quite a pimped-up ride. His Jag had a cream exterior, a tan leather interior and spoilers. It had 'drug dealer' written all over it! I'm not up on cars but it wasn't the XJS he had pinned to his notice boards for the last 30 years. But I've never seen a man more proud. He loved it. I dutifully took the piss and told him to park it on the next street. What would the neighbours think?

Christmas comes around again. Dad is spending the festive season in Scotland with his new fiancée and her family. My new in-laws to be. That's going to be weird – my friend was going to be my new step-sister. What have I done?

I speak to Dad on the 28th, the second anniversary of Mum' s death. He says he's not feeling too good and has decided to stay in bed. Two days later, my friend calls me in a right state.

'The ambulance is here. It's… it's all…it's not good, Sam, he's, he's...' She can't get the words out.

'Are you trying to tell me my Dad is dead?' I start laughing and have to tell her I'll call her back!

I'm in hysterics. I'm laughing so loud, I'm crying. It's not appropriate, but this is how I react to shock. My kids come downstairs and wonder what the heck's going on. In between bouts of hysteria, I tell them that their grandad has died. I can't believe it and, once I've calmed down, I call my friend back.

She tells me he'd been in bed one minute and then fell onto the floor the next. They had tried to resuscitate him. They called the ambulance, but nothing could be done. I can't believe it. Here we go again. Happy New Year!

2010

It is early January and, as my Dad died in another country (Scotland, really?), we have to wait two weeks before his body can be repatriated. The death certificate arrives: an aneurysm.

I'm sad, again. But Dad's death doesn't pierce me like Mum's did. Maybe I'd sensed it might happen. He'd been glued together over the years by a heavy dose of caffeine, nicotine, sugar and Rennies. It's a shock, but not really a surprise.

Bigger changes are afoot this time. The house would have to be sold, there's the will to sort out, his business to close and the Jag to sell. That might prove tricky!

The next year flies by as I'm up and down the country like a yo-yo. I like that part. I feel connected to my Lancashire roots once again. I spend more time there with family and friends than I have in years.

We eventually sell the house, distribute its contents and close down his business. The Jag goes straight away: there's clearly a demand for the pimped-up ride!

Inevitably, the time comes to leave our family home for good. It's going to be weird. I dig up some plants that look like they might survive the trip back to London. I like the idea that something my Mum had planted might continue in my garden.

Although I'd grown up in six different houses, this house is the one with the most memories for me. It isn't a pretty house, nor is it full of beautiful things. Mum and Dad weren't rich. Dad had only recently made some money – hence the Jag – but before that, for many years, they were simply trying to make ends meet.

Clearing the last bit of junk out of the house, I find a plastic toy soldier in a drawer. Probably one of my brother's from years ago. I put him on the top shelf in the porch and lock the door for the final time. The soldier is armed with a gun, positioned to shoot if anyone dares to break in. His job is to guard the house until the new people move in, which turns out to be two years later. He serves us well.

New Beginnings

I really do need to get out of my wallowing and do something productive with my life, something new, something different, something challenging. I think the combination of being a full-time Mum and dealing with my losses was getting me down. I needed a change – but what?

Enter the cavalry. Jheni.
'Coffee?'

We sit in my local coffee shop for hours. By the time we've finished chatting, Jheni's managed to persuade me to get off my backside and apply to go to art college. Don't ask!

'Come on,' she says, 'the deadline for applications is Friday, get a shift on'.

I reluctantly go home and download a personal statement form for Chelsea College of Arts. Well, I'm not doing much else and it's a nice distraction from domesticity. What could I lose?

Once I have procrastinated and tried out some avoidance strategies (mainly of the eating variety), I sit at my computer and make a start. I haven't given it much thought and, as I don't really fancy art college, I decide I might as well be a bit provocative. Well that's what artists do, isn't it?

I surprise myself with what I muster up. Somewhere in the recesses of my brain I manage to unearth something. I tell them how I found myself in an old converted Lancashire mill in Oswaldtwistle (that name always arouses attention as no one can ever pronounce it, unless you're from there) buying cheap art canvasses, delighting at the opportunity to express my inner artist. Adding shock value where I can, I write the biggest load of twaddle. I know I'm being provocative but I don't really care. I'm quite enjoying myself. I finish rambling, put my application in the five o'

clock post and leave it at that.

At the school gates, Jheni keeps asking me if I've heard anything. I keep telling her no and that I'm not expecting to but I thank her for the kick up the bum as it was a good exercise in giving something new a go.

'I'm praying for you', she says. I think she's off her rocker.

A few days later there's a letter on the mat. *'Please bring your portfolio to Chelsea College of Arts at 10am on 12th April'*. Bugger. What am I going to do now – rise to the challenge and see it as a sign, or turn it down and continue with my domestic drudgery?

I don't have a portfolio and I'm not even sure what one is. The last thing I'd drawn was in 1984 for my Art 'O' Level. It was a picture of Annie Lennox copied from the front cover of Smash Hits. Hardly on trend!

I decide to put my fate in the lap of the gods. I call Jheni, 'I need a portfolio'.

'You see, I told you I was praying for you', she laughs, then gives me a 'To Do' list. 'Take your camera and go to every art gallery and museum. Take photos, lots and lots of photos, write something, draw something, you need to create some sketchbooks. Go on, go, get on with it, and be AUDACIOUS, you've only got six weeks!' Jheni is so enthusiastic that it's hard to refuse, so for the next few weeks I go here, there and everywhere. It's like Blue Peter all over again: sticking, cutting, gluing and more importantly, I'm having fun. I go to all the obvious London galleries: Tate Modern & Britain, The National & Portrait Galleries, Saatchi, Whitechapel and more, although I have no clue what I'm supposed to be looking for.

I take a trip north to see my brother and nip into The Storey Gallery in Lancaster. I find myself looking at an art installation about the plight of illegal immigrants and the tragedy of the Chinese cockle pickers at Morecambe Bay. It's very moving. I'm starting to get it. The penny is dropping. Art is an expression of something that we haven't necessarily got the words for. Look at me with all my new-found artiness. Some of the stuff still washes straight over me but other works make me think. Bingo! My brain is starting to light up.

We go on a family weekend to Glastonbury. We're at the Chalice Well and wait in line with all the other tourists, sleeves rolled up ready to fill a bottle of sacred

water from the stream. A few days later back home, I'm looking for something. I take a book from the shelf. As I do, another falls open by my feet. It reads 'The water from the Chalice Well...'. Then a couple of weeks later and I'm with Jheni at yet another exhibition at Tate Britain. There's hundreds of tiny bottles of holy water from all over the world, including the Chalice Well, all beautifully displayed in cabinets and, when I go to get a tissue from my pocket to blow my nose, wrapped up inside it is my Chalice Well bottle of sacred water. I'd forgotten it was there. It's a sign! A sign of what? I have no idea, but I like it.

A few days later I'm at Chelsea with Jheni. She's a student there and I occasionally help her move stuff about. Today, she's changing studios. There's a lot of shifting and lifting required. I'm having one of my repetitive singing days, you know the sort, when you sing the same song over and over again, annoying everyone, especially yourself. Well, today's song is 'Sabbath Prayer' from 'Fiddler on the Roof'. Not one that naturally rolls off the tongue, but it's a song I've sung for the past 25 years, on and off; it had been ingrained during an old school production. There I am, intermittently singing the same first verse over and over whilst we do the packing. When we finally finish, Jheni says 'Take one of my paintings for helping me', and she hands me a small box of about 100 postcard-size paintings. They are all so nice I can't decide. Eventually I get down to six, then two (I know, right, she could have said 'Take both'!). 'Ip dip...' I choose a green and black stripy one, not my usual colours but there's something about it I like. I turn over the card and guess what? She's given names to all her paintings and she's called that one 'Sabbath Prayer'. So you see I'm clearly well on my way to becoming a Chelsea art student. All the signs say so!

In the meantime I have Jackson Pollocked my way around a few of my aforementioned cheap canvasses, and completed six sketchbooks and I now have a portfolio of sorts.

The day arrives. I get to the college with three massive canvasses that I've chucked a bit of paint on and swirled around with a dish cloth. I don't care and I'm having fun. It's like the X Factor and there are hundreds of us. We're all asked to leave our work and come back in an hour. If your name is on the list, you stay for an interview; if not, leave. I'm not sure what's happening, but my emotions are all over the place. I am tearful and have no idea why. Maybe it's all

the expectation. To add to it I have an overwhelming feeling that my Mum is about – her energy, that is, I don't see any flies this time.

The list goes up. My name is on it! Now I really am in trouble. I know absolutely nothing about art, or artists. I can't talk the talk. I feel sick. Luckily, I've dragged Jheni along. We have just one hour to prepare.

The last time I was interviewed was over 20 years ago. Jheni force feeds me art school food while I garble and splutter at the very idea of having to negotiate my way through an interview. It's one thing writing twaddle and chucking a bit of 'oil on canvas' here and there, but talking face to face with people who can smell the deception? I wasn't so sure.

It's my turn. I sit in front of two arty bigwigs and the questions come rolling in. 'Why do you want to be an artist?', 'What's your motivation?' I don't know and I haven't got one, but I can't say that. Thankfully Jheni has prepped me well. 'Be provocative', she said. I drop in a few new names I've picked up whilst wandering around galleries, like Joseph Beuys and Susan Hiller, but that can always catch you out. They may be famous in their world but, if you're just dipping your toe in, any blatant bullshit is easy to spot.

My brain is whizzing, looking for anything that sounds vaguely arty and interesting. I watched a programme the night before about Tolstoy so I mention that, and my uncle had just been to a Grayson Perry exhibition and bought me a tea towel. So I talk about merchandising art: the material world versus authentic art. I am squirming inside at my audacity.

I then turn the pages of my portfolio – and I use that term very lightly – to a photo of my Mum's diaries (I'd found them in a shoe box at the back of her wardrobe when I was clearing out the house). I'd taken an abstract photo in a way that I'd seen on one of my many gallery trips. I talk about the diaries for a minute or two, then the interviewers give each other a look. It was a look that said, 'Yes, we'll have her!'. It was crystal clear that they were going to offer me a place.

Two weeks later, I still hadn't heard anything and everything is closing for Easter. I ring the college to check.

'Oh yes, everyone has had their letters', says the voice on the other end of the phone. Well, I haven't!

'Let me go and see. It's most unusual. I sent them all out myself last week'.

The lady comes back to the phone. 'You're right', she says, 'Yours is still here,

and there's a Post-It note on it with a question mark. That's most odd'.

To be honest the whole three months had been odd, with too many weird and wonderful happenings. But for it all to end with a big fat question mark?

The next day I got a standard letter saying 'thanks, but no thanks' and that was the oddest thing. I was sure this whole experience was guiding me somewhere. I'd instinctively felt they were going to offer me a place and, although I knew art school wasn't really for me, why had I got this far? I spend the next few weeks wondering what it's all been about and the significance of the question mark.

After a lot of thought and reflection on my surreal art experience, I concluded that the whole process had been all about questions: 'What's next?, Who am I?, Where am I going?, What am I doing and why?' Questions I don't have answers to but one thing was crystal clear: a change was coming. I needed to find a way to make myself become 'unstuck'. No-one was going to do it for me. I had to get myself out of the sticky comfort zone that I'd been squelching around in for way too long.

I needed to make connections, not just with other people but with myself and the signs in my universe. Maybe I was having my mid-life crisis?

Mum's Diaries

When I came across my Mum's diaries a few weeks ago, I thought they'd have all the answers to my questions. I thought I'd hit the jackpot. A treasure chest of fascinating facts about my Mum's life packed with wisdom that would surely help me through my own life. Secretly, I thought, I'm sorted!

Not exactly. Her diaries consisted of 30 years of bad weather (well, she did live 'up north'), hairdos, moans and groans and everyday tittle-tattle. There was nothing deep. No Gandhi-style mantras or philosophical quotes. The diaries were not what I'd expected. They seemed a bit nondescript. Disappointingly, there were no juicy bits or hidden secrets. Well, apart from her very first diary, dated 1972. A diary so small it was hard to read the contents, but it was of particular interest to me.

I think Mum initially took up her pen to purge. She'd got pregnant with my sister at 18, married young and then had me. By the time my Mum and Dad both reached 25, the cracks had set in. She was suspicious my Dad was up to no good – and she was right. It was the beginning of the end. For the rest of that year she scribbled away the heartache and the practicalities of going through a break-up. One of her first entries was 'August 17th 1972: He said he was leaving me!' To be fair it was probably all a bit too much, too young.

She didn't write again until 1983. Eleven years on, by which time we'd moved house four times and changed school three, she'd re-married so I now had a step dad. They'd had my brother and opened a business. It had been a busy time.

What had I expected in her diaries? Well, selfishly I thought she might have written about us. Weren't we the be all and end all of her life? I did think she would have at least mentioned my school ski trip to Bulgaria. That trip was definitely worth a diary entry: I ended up in hospital! I'll fill you in.

There was an incident on the plane when another girl, Mandy Ashworth, and I were taken ill. To this day, I'm not sure what we were ill with exactly but it was like a scene from the film 'Airplane'. Had we had the chicken or the fish? A drama unfolded. Six passengers from first class were asked to give up their

seats so two 14-year-old girls could lie down and be put on oxygen. There were discussions that we might have to land in what was then still Yugoslavia. Thankfully, we made it to Bulgaria. It was all very dramatic. We were greeted on the runway by an ambulance that swiftly 'nee naw-ed' us through Lada-strewn traffic jams on through the grey, icy streets of Sofia to the hospital.

Bulgaria was still a communist country back then. As we entered the hospital on our stretchers, a body was being wheeled out on another. There were thick, blood-stained concrete walls with gaping holes, likely relics of the Soviet era. We were ushered into a tiny consulting room, crammed with doctors, all smoking. It was scary and surreal. Mandy and I lay half-naked being poked and prodded. Then, finding nothing wrong, they injected us with goodness knows what into our bottoms for good measure and started to barter with us for our 'sexy underwear'. Coincidentally, we were both wearing matching M&S bra and knicker sets in burgundy satin which were probably on trend back home, but not in Bulgaria. They were very keen to relieve us of our underwear. Thankfully our teacher was firm and we left, lingerie intact. It was a memorable trip.

A week later back home when I told Mum what had happened, she knew. She said she'd told my Dad at the exact same time that it was all kicking off, 'There's something not right, Samantha's not well, there's something not right, I can feel it'. It was a time when communication wasn't instant. There was no way she would have found out until I got home and told her. That was just one of many sympathetic pains we shared. I don't know what they call it – psychic, psychosomatic, paranormal? Who knows, but when I was pregnant years later, she went through labour pains with me, 250 miles away. And, when she had cancer and, unbeknownst to me, was losing her ability to walk, I woke one morning to find that my legs wouldn't work. It was scary. I couldn't move and the pain was unbearable. I rang Mum and she told me what she was experiencing. Although we weren't a gushy lot, our bond was strong, sometimes too strong and painful. So you'd think she might have noted down some of our weird synchronicities but nope, not a jot!

After my initial disappointment, I decided to re-read her diaries. It was then I realised that there was a wealth of information and insight into her life. They

might not have contained sensational psychic experiences, gossip and drama, but, in her one – line entries, she covered most topics that many people experience at some point in their lives. She had penned years of the everyday and I found them quite funny.

Mum's diaries ran continuously until a few days before she died in December 2007. They didn't navel gaze, no dramas, just statements of fact. I don't think it was intentional, but they were all very deadpan and I could hear her saying every one of her entries.

The more I read Mum's words the more I was gripped. Unwittingly she was describing life in quick one-liners; general observations of what was going on around her and what she was up to. 'April 8th 1983: Planted Gladioli', 'May 7th 1998: Phyllis is coughing up blood', 'September 28th 2002: The neighbours left a tap dripping with the plug in for a fortnight, what a mess!' They reminded me of Alan Bennett in their delivery.

The weather came up most days; 'July 29th 1998: Worst summer for years, RAIN!'. There were births; '30th April: Gemma arrived', deaths; 'March 23rd 1987: They found Mrs Greenhalgh in the canal!' and marriages; 'February 10th 2005: Prince Charles to marry Camilla, as if we care'.

Then there was her hair obsession; 'November 23rd 1987: My hair needs doing, badly!' and times when she was in low moods; 'December 31st 2003: First New Year at home alone. DULL is the operative word!'. The television was the bane of her life; 'March 17th 1999: Do we really have to watch the telly, EVERY night?' And there were fun nights out with her friends; 'January 9th 2004: Went out to the ladies club, played dominoes, laughter is the best medicine'.

There were car issues; 'March 26th 1998: The suspension's gone again' as well as the taking umbrage with Mr Blair and his politics; 'September 7th 2000: Petrol is a big problem, will Blair back down? I can't go anywhere I have NO petrol'.

Sometimes there were money troubles; 'May 10th 1998: Bank bouncing cheques' and holidays in countries that no longer exist; 'June 17th 1988: Maureen and Alec off to Yugoslavia'.

There were good times; 'June 7th 1997: Richard found 10k in the back of an old desk, can this be real? It's fantastic!', and drunken times; 'July 15th 1984: Went to the pub, I was a bit gassed'.

She records the never ending stream of appointments: 'October 23rd 1987:

Dentist, three fillings and a polish – £70'. 'April 19th 2000: The dreaded smear', and 'September 14th 2001: Eye sight is getting worse, need new glasses. Must make an appointment'.

Over 30 years of writing, she covered most of what life throws at us, especially for women. Her impenetrable hormones; 'July 24th 1993: Bad, bad period pain, now 59 days heavy', and her need for space & freedom; 'February 12th 2004: I need to get out of here, I have no space!'

There is something comforting in knowing that we're all doing the same things day in day out, punctuated by life-changing events. I've come to realise this is what connects us and I was missing my connection. I needed something to 'fix' me. Everything I'd known as stable and secure had gone. I know it all sounds a bit dramatic, being that I'm a grown woman with three children of my own, but I really missed my Mum and I was at a loss.

There's more of Mum's diary entries at the bottom of each page in Part Two.

Momentary Lapse of Reason

What was my passion though – my focus? I was busy enough with the kids and daily life, but I needed an injection of something stimulating and different. I have a brain and it needs using. I was in limbo. I needed Mum's guidance but she wasn't there anymore.

I had read somewhere that frustration is just gestation dying to get out and thankfully, one day, I simply popped. An idea came to me and it felt good. If I was missing the main woman in my life, why didn't I seek solace from those that were still here? What would it be like to talk a bit more in-depth to other women, to listen to and learn from their experiences? And not just two or three, maybe lots of women? Wouldn't it be rather lovely to spend some time slowing right down and getting to know more about my friends and acquaintances? I started to wonder how deeply we talk to each other anymore? I mean real conversations not just offloading or catching up, but telling each other our deepest thoughts and listening to each other? I found a quote which seemed to sum up my thinking;

'What happened to a world in which we can sit with the people we love so much and have slow conversations about the state of our heart and soul, conversations that slowly unfold, conversations with pregnant pauses and silences that we are in no rush to fill?'
from 'The Disease of Being Busy', by Omid Safi.

I began telling people I was starting a project about women and would they like to spend some time talking to me? Once I had said it, I knew I couldn't back down. So there it was. I had a quest.

People asked me, 'How many women are you going to talk to?' I hadn't thought about it but then, if I didn't have a goal, I might never reach it. I came up with a number. One hundred!

'Bloody hell, that's a lot of women. What are you going to do with the information?' I was asked. I was on a roll and, in a momentary lapse of reason, I flippantly said, 'Oh I'm writing a book!' Well, I did say I needed a challenge.

Interviewing 100 women and writing a book. Nothing like throwing yourself in at the deep end.

My plan was hatched. I now just needed some questions.

For 30 years Mum wrote practically and, at the same time, viscerally, about what makes for a human life. In just a few words she marked an occasion, a real day, a practical problem or an observation. Her diaries seeded some ideas in me.

My plan was to ask these women how they 'do life'. I wanted to see how they felt about the reality of everyday life. The nitty gritty, the stuff we all do day in, day out, but don't necessarily stop to think or talk about.

Finally, I had something that I felt passionate about; getting into deep conversations and lifting up the rocks to see what's underneath. When can I start?

Collecting Conversations

2011

It's mid-June. Armed with my questions, I'm ready. Obviously Jheni is my first 'victim'. We sit at my kitchen table for most of the day. I ask her my questions and we weave through many aspects of her life.

I've known Jheni a long time but how well do I actually know her? Today she describes herself as a 'cackling, green tea drinking, bibliophile'. As you've heard previously, Jheni is one of the most enthusiastic people I know. Croydon–born, of Jamaican heritage. Full of passion and encouragement. Single Mum to three and an eternal student. She's always learning. It's her life blood, that and prayer, 'Thanks be to God'.

I didn't intend the day to be quite so ritualistic but we ended up drinking Matcha tea (posh green tea used in Japanese tea making ceremonies) and eating freshly baked chocolate cake that I rustled up mid-conversation. It turns out to be a really lovely day, sort of old-fashioned. There were no agendas and, for once, no-one had to be anywhere. It was very healing.

Five hours later, having covered an array of topics and we are all talked out, she turns the table right back on me and says, 'Now you have to ask for feedback. You need to hear what this process is doing, so, go on, ask me...' I squirm and reluctantly ask, 'What have you taken from doing this today?' She replies, 'I didn't expect this illumination about myself, it's the best time you'll spend, it's precious and valuable. Thank God for this time. There's something angelic, healing and caring about this process'.

Wow! What an accolade, and an affirmation that what I was doing might serve some good.

One down. 99 to go.

A couple of days later I bump in to Alice, an elderly woman who lives on my street. We initially met a few years ago in sad and unusual circumstances. We had another neighbour, George, who lived with his agoraphobic, bed-bound sister. He was a private old-fashioned gentleman, the sort who'd tilt his trilby and say 'Good morning'. I would occasionally bump into him at Sainsbury's but it wasn't unusual for me not to see him from one week to the next. Other than that, I knew nothing about him. One morning, there was a swarm of people dressed head-to-foot in white overalls and carrying chemical spray-pumps outside his house. I wondered what had happened. It didn't look good. It wasn't. It was awful.

I later found out that George had had a heart attack, fallen down the stairs and died. He'd been lying there for five weeks before anyone realised and, even more tragically, his sister had died in bed from starvation. It was horrible. It transpired that they had no friends or relatives and were literally left to rot. It was only when new neighbours moved in and found they were infested with flies, maggots and a terrible smell that it become apparent what had happened.

After the funeral – two coffins side-by-side and a congregation of six – a small group of neighbours came together. That's when I met Alice and a few other elderly people who live close by. We swapped phone numbers and promised to keep an eye out for each other; our own little neighbourhood watch.

Over the years since, I've got to know Alice quite well. I pop in to see her at least once a week. She's fiercely independent. She's lived by herself since her ageing parents died, forty-odd years ago. I don't have a lot of experience with the elderly and she's quite shy, so I'm surprised when she agrees to be interviewed for my project.

I start with my opener, 'How are you, Alice?', hoping to see where my rather open-ended question will lead. She replies with, 'Sometimes being with other people makes me feel a bit flat and I feel overwhelmed. I like my own space'. My second interview and I am already being challenged. Not everyone cares to share their lives in the detail I thought that they might. People might appear lonely but, in fact, they like their life for the simplicity and quietness it brings.

I am grabbing time whenever I can to listen. It's not easy or nearly as straightforward as I'd thought it was going to be and, by the end of the first year, I've only done 11 interviews. Why did I say I'd do 100? Maybe I had over-egged the pudding. I bump into a friend on the tube who tells me for his PhD he is interviewing 25 people and he's finding it all a bit stressful! Hmm!

Christmas comes and goes and just before everyone heads back to school we decide to take leave of our senses and head off to Cornwall for some surfing. It's frigging freezing. One morning, on a coastal walk into St Ives, something strange happens. I start running. I hate running, and I mean hate it. But I run. I run up the coastline, in normal shoes, in a big hat and coat. I just take off and I can't stop. I'm like Forrest Gump. It's weird: up hill, down hill and I'm not out of breath, I'm not even complaining. I don't stop. It's freeing, liberating, like there's something stuck inside me that has to come out. I haven't done it again since and it's very out of character. I must have looked a right sight, but it releases something. I come home renewed.

2012

It's January. Having done the school run I've invited Caris round. She is a local nanny in her early 30s. She's from Jamaican heritage, a born and bred Londoner.

Almost immediately she tells me about her grandfather who she was particularly close to. And although he died when she was 15, her memories of him are strong. She tells me how much she still misses him and how he was a natural man, the glue to their family. She explains how they used to go off and sit for hours and hours and simply chat. Music to my ears. He had a lot of time for people and many words of wisdom. We chatted for most of the day about all sorts of topics but somehow it's the simplicity of her sitting with her grandad that paints such a wonderful image.

The weather is chilly and Alice phones to tell me her house isn't warm. I pop round to bleed her radiators. We get chatting and she announces that she'll be 90 in a few weeks. I ask her if she'd like to do something special, maybe a lunch party? She likes the idea and four weeks later, I host a lunch party for 12 ladies who between them have lived for over 1,000 years!

My husband, who is called Martin by the way, is turning 50 soon and has always wanted to go to Barbados. I've inherited a bit of money so I book a week in April for the five of us. We only go and miss the flight! Just two miles away from the airport we hit the longest traffic jam ever. Reports are coming in on the radio that a taxi driver has run someone over at the drop-off area. The whole area is closed off as it is now a crime scene. Inevitably we miss our flight. Later we're told we won't be able to get a flight for another two days so, instead of heading home, we opt for Brighton as it's just down the road. It's wet, windy and freezing – not exactly the 30 degree temperatures we were hoping for. We eventually make it to Barbados for a very brief four days only to find everything is closed for the Easter weekend!

Most of the Spring is taken over by swimming competitions. In the swimming calendar this is the busiest time of year. We trundle off weekly to various leisure centres scattered around the South East to endure a day of perpetual warmth and dehydration. I had hoped Connie would have given up by now. I know I should encourage her but being surrounded by a bunch of overly-competitive parents isn't my idea of fun. It's certainly eye-opening; they're more competitive than the kids.

The year is flying by and it's May already. We've just spent the weekend in the Yorkshire Dales for my niece's 21st birthday. We stay outside the village of Dent in a youth hostel, not far from the Lake District. It's a beautiful setting and it's even sunny! There are miles and miles of green fields and sitting tall in the middle of it all are the arches of the Ribblehead Viaduct. It's a sight for sore eyes, as is my biological father, who turned up after an absence of forty years. But that's definitely another story!

Back home and I'm arranging my next interview. I've managed 30 so far.

My next interview is with passionate opera singer Philippa. Recently widowed she tells me what happened. She was on a train from Clapham to Croydon when her phone went. It was her husband. He was in Battersea at the local Homebase. 'He told me he wasn't feeling well and I instantly knew something was wrong', she said. 'He had a heart attack, I couldn't get off the train, I knew I couldn't get to

him. That was the last time we spoke'.

In such awful circumstances it's easy to see how people left behind can get fed up with life. But Philippa is a positive woman with a strong faith. Now a single Mum of two, she reflects by saying that the time she had with her husband is untouchable. It's in a box and she can open that box anytime she wants to. I love her philosophy and feel privileged that she wanted to be one of my 100 women.

A few years back, I remember having one of those warm feelings when you know all is well with the world. I'd dropped the kids off at school and went back to one of the mum's for coffee. There I met close friends Ana from Serbia and Nadia from Bosnia. We had coffee and a wedge of homemade Serbian curd cake and, after discussing the ingredients that make up this weird and, if I'm honest, quite difficult to digest cake, we started talking about the war. Both women had come to England to leave the madness behind. Nadia told me her brother-in-law had been killed by a Serbian. It would have been easy to see how these two women could have been at loggerheads and not become the best of friends. That conversation was a joy to be part of; cake, conversations of conflict and friendship in the same room. Women world peacemakers – there's a thought!

When you spend time listening, uninterrupted and have quality time with people, it is cathartic. I'm learning a lot. People say it's the small things that make a difference and it really is. So many people I asked to take part said, 'You don't want to talk to me, I have nothing to say. I'm boring'. I find the total opposite. I'm realising that we're all essentially made from the same mixture, just with different toppings.

You know when I said the swimming club was full of overly-competitive parents? Well it seems I have got myself an overly-competitive daughter. She managed to qualify for the Nationals by the skin of her £230 swimming costume (how much?). Me and the kids head off to Sheffield for a week to watch two races that last less than 50 seconds! Thankfully that was her goal and having reached it, my seven years of being a swimming mum are finally over.

Summer's here and I down tools.

September brings the usual last-minute uniform and shoe buying. Aaaand breathe! Everyone is back to where they should be and I can begin again.

I've arranged for Laura to come round. She is a mum that I met at the school gate. I learn she's a stacker…she puts the shopping away in perfect order. The fridge is stacked in exactly the same way week in week out. Everything has its place and woe betide anyone who messes it up. She calls herself a fridge freak. She's also shoe-obsessed and recently had shelves specially made so she can stack her 130-pair collection in order of preference, with her faves on the top shelf and so on. She shows me a photo of them on her phone. I've never seen anything like it. I wear the same pair of shoes until they fall off me. Women's idiosyncrasies are all so weirdly wonderful.

As half-term looms, I'm nearly 40 women down and 60 to go.

There's a World Market Day at my son, James' primary school. It's one of those days when you feel good to be alive. There's a real sense of community and coming together. The day is orchestrated by Rachel, one of the teachers. She gathers as many people as she can and asks them to bring food from their heritage. There are about 30 stands each serving food from all around the globe. It's beautiful, interesting, tasty and the smells are mouth-watering.

Rachel is from Lancashire. I feel a pull towards her. We bond over the Eccles cakes and both agree that our stall is not for the faint-hearted. There's meat and potato pie with mushy peas, Lancashire hotpot, Chorley cakes, Parkin, Lancashire cheese and black pudding. Thankfully nobody brought tripe. I was tempted to bring along some chip butties, but I think there's already enough stodge to warrant our own defibrillator and to rename the day 'World Carb Day!'

A couple of weeks later Rachel and I are sat at my kitchen table. It is another delightful day. We talk about her dad. He died a couple of years ago at the grand age of 91. Her connection with him was very strong and she misses him terribly. She tells me he was a warm supportive man who was interested in her and her family. He was a man who would listen and give of his time. She is left with some lovely memories but says that when it happened and, for quite a while after, she felt lost. With the passage of time she's found herself making bigger life decisions, becoming more independent and even getting on better with her sister, something her dad told her would happen.

The Christmas holidays are looming and, as usual, there's always too much to do to fit into such a small window of time. Why do we all have to see each other before Christmas? What's wrong with January, the most boring month of the year?

2013

It's been two years since I had that kick up the backside coffee with Jheni. She's introduced me to a friend of hers, Barbara. I don't know her at all. She's riddled with arthritis and finds it difficult to get out, so I go and collect her. I love her right away. What a fabulous woman, so open. She's had her fair share of troubles. Something she told me hits me in the solar plexus each time I reread this, '…he loved the girls, and the fist' – thankfully that was years ago and now aged 69 she's happily married to her second husband and content with her lot. She offers good advice, 'Friends – listen to them, hear what they have to say'. I couldn't agree more.

Routine is punctuated with school holidays, meal times, trips to the dentist and don't get me started on verrucas. Twice-monthly appointments to gouge fungal infested feet. Kids, who'd have 'em?

By the end of the summer term I've spoken to 65 women. We break for the summer and venture to France for our holidays.

Here comes the fly, she's back…

Connie had gone a week earlier to stay with a friend in another part of France. We arrange to meet them in Nice. Well, that's the plan, but they don't quite make it!

A mile or two after setting off, she starts texting me. Their train has broken down. It's August, it's hot, there's no air-conditioning. They're in third class; I didn't even know there was third class! They have no water. Their French isn't great and no-one seems to speak English. We are still at Gatwick.

Connie keeps texting to update me. Her texts start off quite humorous, commenting on grumpy kids and irritable parents.

A couple of hours later, we arrive in Nice, half-expecting them to be there but their train hadn't moved. Stationary for four hours, the tone of her texts had become more serious. Tempers were fraying. She tells me about a woman who'd

become hysterical, children throwing up and people panicking. Eventually, paramedics are called and a fire engine manages to get onto the tracks and the emergency services break a window to remove an over-heated passenger who'd passed out. I don't think it's quite the adventure of a lifetime that two 16-year-olds were expecting!

Six hours later we eventually find them. Rushing up to us, the first thing my daughter's friend says is, 'You'll never guess what Sam, there was this fly, and it hovered around Connie the whole time. It was weird, right? It must have been your Mum 'coz it didn't fly away. It wasn't buzzy and irritating, it was really calm. We said, "It's your gran", didn't we Con?'

I look at Connie, she nods in agreement. Wow! I'm glad they had a distraction for the hours they were stuck, but I was knackered and, to be honest, I'm not paying as much attention as I should. I just wanted to get us settled into our villa.

The next morning, I feel a need to process the previous day as it had been a bit full on. I find a quiet spot in the garden, get my phone and start scrolling through the texts. No sooner had I started than a fly lands on my screen and doesn't budge until I finish. Weird!

A month later and everybody's back to school. Routine starts again. I'm asked away on a girls' weekend in Dorset. Yes, please! We head out for dinner on the Saturday night. We are sat chatting in a cosy restaurant when my friend says, 'Look at that fly'. I look up and directly in front of me is a fly on the wall. For some reason I put out my finger and surprisingly on she climbs. I bring my arm down to the middle of the table and tell the girls my story so far. One thing Mum loved more than anything was a girls' weekend away so I wasn't really surprised she showed up. I think she was enjoying all the attention and was in no hurry to leave. Eventually, we ask for the bill and I gently shake her away.

I know a fly is a bit of a weird symbol for your dead Mum. Often people associate robins, white feathers, even butterflies with the dear departed but my mum always said, 'Wouldn't it be fun if you could be a fly on the wall'. Careful what you wish for is what I say! That's not the end of the fly story, though, there's still more to come later…

In October, I head North to do more interviews. Cheryl appears throughout Mum's diaries. Mum would pay her a visit every four to six weeks for 20 odd years. She was Mum's hairdresser. The colours, the perms, the conversations. Mum often commented on how going to Cheryl was like therapy, 'a breath of fresh air'.

Cheryl is down to earth. A woman with a positive disposition. We chat. She tells me how she loves her job. Back in the Seventies in a post-industrial Lancashire village there wasn't a lot of choice. She says it was the factory or hairdressing, so she chose hairdressing and has been doing it ever since. Women go round to 'hers', she puts the kettle on and washes their hair over the kitchen sink. They have a couple of hours of chatting, putting the world to rights, laughing and drinking tea. Sounds like my sort of day.

The next day I meet up with my old school friend, Karen, and head to an old haunt; Swales Café in Clitheroe, famed for its delicious local meat and potato pie and ice cream floats. Full to bursting we then spend the afternoon wandering around Clitheroe Castle reminiscing about all the boys we'd snogged on the bandstand.

I'm now up to 70, not snogs, but women. Seventy interviews, now I know I will finish. I'm on the home stretch.

I come back to London to find that Alice has had a fall. I knew this would happen eventually. Things might have to change for Alice. She's not hurt, more shocked, and her confidence has plummeted. I get involved. Having only ever been on the periphery of her life up until this point, I now know a few things will need sorting out. Decisions to be made and safety measures put in place. I go round for a chat. On closer inspection, I see she's taken to filing things, on the floor! It looks neat enough but, when I help her look for some necessary paperwork, there is more to this than meets the eye. She has mice, and they've settled in. I venture upstairs. Oh Lord, the dust!

After her fall she's finding it difficult to get in and out of bed. She wants to downsize to the box room. It's spartan, just a single bed, a bedside table and a threadbare rug. As I hoover the carpet crumbles, it's fit for nothing. I don't think this room has seen the light of day in 40 years.

The following week I'm at Alice's house every day. We go and choose new carpet. Miraculously, only a few days later, a sea of sunset orange covers the floor. It's certainly a statement piece! One thing leads to another and, before we know it, we've sorted every room and every drawer in the house. It's like an episode of 'The Hoarder Next Door' without the emotional angst.

After a few conversations Alice is now supplied with an emergency alarm, a twice-monthly cleaner and a weekly supply of ready-meals delivered right to her front door. I don't know about her, but I'm feeling much better about the situation.

Another interview today and I'm meeting Gen. She's 77 and I've known her for 25 years. Initially she was one of my clients then we became friends. She's always inspired me. She seeks out adventures and is a keen photographer and artist. She even has her own dark room. Her walls are full of interesting art work. I love going into someone's home and getting a sense of them through their aesthetics.

Whenever she travels, she tries to go by train so she can see more of the landscape around her. We chat. Back when she was in her 20s, she got a job with the Foreign Office. Initially they posted her to Malaysia and a few years later to Benghazi, in Libya. She tells me how she'd owned a horse and used to ride him through the desert with her dog upon the saddle beside her as it wasn't safe for women to venture out alone. I think the very idea of anyone riding a horse across the Sahara desert these days seems like an impossible undertaking. Somehow it feels like life was a bit simpler back then. Her stories certainly paint a more romantic time.

I've now done 85 interviews and I press pause on my project as it's Christmas.

2014

With just 15 interviews left, my data gathering was just that – data. Sooner or later I'd need to figure what to do with it all. How on earth am I supposed to make this into a book? I did say I'd do it, but I'm beginning to regret my brash statement.

Recently, I'd been to see a photography exhibition by Ansel Adams at the National Maritime Museum in Greenwich. It was the most beautiful photography. I bought the book. Still in the bag, it was the only thing on my kitchen table that morning when Dolly came round. Dolly is 94 and from Trinidad and Tobago. An adventurous lady and determined too. Just two years ago she walked the Great Wall of China.

She tells me she came to London in the Fifties on one of the last 'banana boats' from the Caribbean when her husband, a famous boxer of the time, was being promoted in London. I don't know why but I asked her what her husband's name was. 'Ansel Adams', she replied! Flipping 'eck, I reach for the paper bag and pull out the book and showed her. We gave each other a knowing look. The stars were aligning on us that day for sure. She is an amazing woman. I could listen to her all day – and I did.

It's the middle of May, and I'm on a train heading North. With only half a dozen interviews left, I'm heading back to Read to talk with two women I've known most of my life. One is my godmother and my Mum's oldest friend, Cynthia, and the other is my oldest friend's mum, Josie.

It's Saturday lunch time and I nip to the village chippy to get a portion of chips and gravy. Gravy on your chips down south is unheard of, so, whenever I'm back in Read, it's my own nostalgic ritual. I sit on the wall of the laundrette and devour the vinegary gravy, chip combo. I'm in heaven. My Mum would be turning in her grave; she thought it was common to eat in the street.

I wander round to Josie's for our chat. Her daughter and I were like peas in a pod growing up. We became blood sisters (a ritual of both pricking your finger with a pin and rubbing your blood together. Not recommended these days). We'd wear matching clothes, hairstyles and obsess about Starksy and Hutch. I thought Josie was the best mum; whenever I went round to play she'd offer me the tin of biscuits. Posh biscuits, the proper ones. The ones in foil wrappers; the Clubs, Breakaways, and Penguins and if we were really lucky, Trios and Kit-Kats too! We only got plain, boring, digestives at our house. So you can imagine, I'd scoff as many as I could.

The next day I head round to Cynthia's house. Obviously we talked about Mum a lot; after all they'd shared memories of over 50 years. We get out old photo albums and reminisce. There were a few tears. Laughing, she says, 'I'm not comfortable with people whose bladders are too close to their eyes'. It took me a while to work out what she meant. Public displays of grief!

Cyn's a wise woman. 'Nobody promises it's all singing and dancing, you know. You have to appreciate the boringness of life. There's a few people who live round here that are quite content searching out a good old pot of chutney. Some people think they're boring, but they're not, they're just content'. I've lived down south so long I had forgotten the straight talking, no-nonsense, down-to-earth approach to life that northerners are famed for. It's reassuringly refreshing.

Back home and I'm speeding along to my penultimate interview. It's with Gillian. Talk about coincidences and signs, this one has to be up there. I met Gillian at the buffet breakfast whilst we were on our four-day holiday to Barbados a couple of years ago. I'd overheard her talking and her accent sounded familiar. I started up with, 'Where's that accent from?' to which she replied, 'Bury, in Lancashire'. Just around the corner from my Mum. I told her about Read, then she said, 'My Mum used to live there. She died a couple of years ago'. I asked the whereabouts and I knew exactly where. Coincidently Cheryl and Josie were her neighbours. She told me her Mum's name was Anne. I didn't know her – that would have been a sign too far – but I have a suspicion my Mum would have. I later found out Mum had in fact taken Anne on a ladies outing to a Christmas pantomime.

I told Gillian about my project and we swapped phone numbers, which led to me driving down to her beautiful home in Surrey. We spend the afternoon sat outside on her terrace overlooking the countryside. I've found my dream job just as I'm ending it.

Only one interview left, but it isn't going to happen straight away, as the summer holidays are upon us again. But I am going to have to knuckle down and get some writing done.

September and the fly's back...

I haven't seen any sign of my fly for a year or so until today. I'm at home, sat at the kitchen table, messing about on Facebook. I look down on the floor and see this enormous fly. I put my hand down and she walks onto my finger. This has happened twice now and it's weird, flies don't normally do this; ladybirds, yes, flies, no! I bring her up to the table. She gets off and has a wander around. As she climbs back up my hand, I grab my phone and take some photos. I need evidence for this overfamiliar fly! I then take her upstairs to show to the kids.

I go into Anna's room, she is dutifully sat at her desk doing homework. I say, 'Your gran's come to say 'hi'. Look!' The fly flies off my hand, circles the room and lands on the desk. I put my finger out and, once again, back up she climbs. This is surreal, but I'm getting used to it. I then take her into the bathroom, where James is about to shower. It's hot and noisy. Wouldn't any normal fly buzz off at this point? 'Look, look', I say, 'it's your gran'. He looks vaguely interested. I then take her to Connie's room. 'Here's granny!' in a similar manner to Jack Nicholson in the Shining. She just raises her eyebrows as if to say, 'Loser'.

I go back downstairs with 'Mum' still attached. I sit back at my computer and wonder what I should do with her. I start to type and eventually she flies away. I glance at the calendar on my computer. It's hard to believe, but it's the 8th of September – Mum's birthday.

So, the signs are back. I'm not sure what they are telling me, but they give me encouragement to carry on with my project. Whenever I feel stuck and want to forget it all and get myself a 'proper' job, I get a sign.

The fly story isn't quite over…

My Diaries

2014

Like Mum, I keep diaries, too. However, mine are even less detailed than hers were. In fact, mine really are 'To Do' lists. After all, I wouldn't want to miss any verruca appointments! But, for some clarity of mind, I've decided to use my diaries to purge my ever-increasing frustrations about how to write this book.

September 8th: Mum's birthday. So far, I've created a lever arch file jammed packed full of stories, all in illegible handwriting. Someone did say to me I should have recorded them – but that hindsight stuff is hard to come by!

September 9th: I start to write my book. But procrastination quickly sets in. I don't know what I'm doing. Talking about it and doing it are two different things, and I seem to talk about it, a lot. I'm now wondering where I should write my book, what paper to use, what font to use. The phone's ringing, as is the door bell, and the fridge is beckoning me to find inspiration in there. There's yet another school form to fill in on the kitchen table. I hate forms! This is no good. I'm way too easily distracted. I can't do it. I don't even know where to start.

Ever the practical, over the next few weeks I busy myself by making four almost identical scrapbooks. Back to Blue Peter days. I cut, stick and glue extracts from all my interviews and put them into the scrapbooks. I make them look pretty and even back them with material. I might be enjoying myself but this isn't writing a book. I'm kidding myself. I'm realising what I have always been told, 'Samantha is easily distracted'.

October 6th: I meet up with a friend and tell her my frustrations. She tells me I need structure! Nope, no idea what she's talking about. I hear what she's saying, but it makes no sense to me.

I might have bitten off more than I can chew – and did I mention I can only two-finger type? Most words need re-typing by the end of a sentence, so the typing alone is taking twice as long as it should. I can't seem to generate order to my words and thoughts. I spew it all out and it doesn't make any sense. Moaning is a wonderful distraction. If I ever reach the end, I will have gone through just about every ailment, condition and excuse in the book. Just get on with it.

October 13th: First time I am enjoying myself today. It's interesting to see how different days unfold. One day out of six weeks, not bad!

October 15th: Spoke too soon. Why do I feel so awkward? I'm uncomfortable and I don't know why. I think it's because I think I'm wasting my time. I should get a proper job and stop this nonsense right now.

October 17th: Number 100! My last interview, but it's a long one. I travel to Pam's house in Chiswick. She lives in a beautiful house, right on the River Thames. I'm in awe. I'm like a child in a sweet shop. Not only is it situated in one of London's most scenic places but her house is steeped in history. Her family have lived there for generations and it's full of charm and character. Funnily enough we don't finish the interview. It's got nothing to do with me nosing around her house for hours, honest!

It's funny how I've almost finished my project but seem to be dragging it out. I tell myself that, whilst I'm still interviewing, I'm still doing research and therefore don't have to 'write' my book. I see where this is going…

October 20th: I go to Sainsbury's. Whilst loading my shopping at the till, the checkout lady starts telling me, 'It's took me 20 years to find a reason to leave him, I've done it. It's brilliant, everything is lovely, my house is lovely, everyone says how much lighter I am. I had to pussyfoot around him, treading carefully, careful as to what I said, now I am free, liberated'. I'm surprised for two reasons: one, that she is telling a random stranger her situation (whilst scanning my carrots!) and two, the fact that she's been in this predicament for years and, finally, she's had the courage to change it. You find inspiration in the most ordinary places!

October 21st: I'm doing more research. Went to see a photographic exhibition about 100 women. Bugger, someone's beaten me to it. You see, procrastination doesn't pay. I admire it, but it wasn't for me. I'm learning that looking at other people's work either inspires me or makes me realise my work is just as valid, and it gives me more confidence to pursue what I'm doing. I bought the exhibition book for research and, I like mine better. Wow, look at me with all that confidence. I'm positively oozing the stuff!

November 4th: Disaster strikes. I pick up my laptop and re-read it all. It's shit and I can't do it. That'll teach me to be so cocky.

2015

January 5th: It's my first day back to it after the Christmas holidays. The kids are all back at school and, OMG, talk about lack of motivation. I can't remember a thing. What was I doing? Where was I heading? Everything has been wiped from my mind. I think I might be menopausal, my brain has retained nothing!

January 8th: Hang on a minute, I've just done another interview. Doesn't that make it 101? Yes, but I haven't finished the last one, and now I've arranged another couple with some more women. Come on Samantha: deadlines!

January 13th: Joined night school. If I'm writing a book I'd better be able to talk about it. I'm trying public speaking. I don't like it, it's scary.

February 15th: Alice said her friend would like to be interviewed. She's 95. How can I refuse? The problem is, the more people I tell, the more I want to talk to them. This could go on forever. I have to stop sometime.

February 27th: My last interview, 107! A day trip to Blackpool. Off to interview Auntie Pauline. We're not related. She's one of Mum's life-long friends. We used to play with her kids when we were little, then you grow up and life takes over and you never see them again. The last time I saw her was at Mum's funeral so today was going to be a proper catch up.

I had no idea of the life she led. There are people that are part of your formative years but you just know them as your Mum's friends. She tells me that as a Catholic girl getting pregnant at 17 meant she was in trouble. Her Mum and doctor told her it would injure her mind to have an abortion so she must have him and then give him away. Whilst pregnant she was sent to live with her aunt to avoid the family shame. The baby arrived. But soon the day came when she had to hand him over. She recalls when the nun carried him off down a corridor, he started to cry. She could hear him crying for ages. She says she can still hear him to this day.

Amazingly, years later when her baby was all grown up and had children of his own, she got him back. He was always in the back of her mind, how could he not be? Although she says having him back was nearly as traumatic as giving him away as there was so much guilt. But now her life is wonderful as he and his family are part of hers.

May 4th: Sent my first draft off last week to be edited. Nearly every sentence is covered in red. It's like being at school all over again. It's my spelling and appalling typing – and as for the punctuation!

June 17th: As I left my house this morning I saw an ambulance in the street. I don't think too much about it. I go out for the day and come back to find that Alice has been taken to hospital. She's becoming a liability to herself. I go and visit her and tell her, nicely, that she is going to have to change her arrangements. Either she gets carers in, goes into a home or gets someone to come and live with her. She spends a week in St Thomas' Hospital under observation. They find nothing wrong but when she comes home she looks like a new woman. She has been looked after, fed and watered properly. She needs help.

Two weeks later she asks me to pop up and see her. 'I don't want to spend another winter here, I think I should go into a home'. Music to my ears. I can't believe how willing and open she is. I spend the next few weeks doing research and we visit six care homes.

July 29th: Summer holidays now, and nothing is going to happen for a while. I feel this writing business isn't really my thing. But I've got to carry on. I've come this far and not to finish it would be a mistake. I still feel there is something missing though.

I just can't put my finger on it. I need someone to help me. Is there such a person?

It's September. Big changes this year. Connie's off to university, Anna's going into sixth form and James starts secondary school. Finally, 14 years of doing the school run are over.

September 8th: Mum would have been 69 today. It's a shame she died so young, we would have had a lot of fun. Life's a lot easier now the kids are older.

September 10th: Alice is trying out a care home for a week, to see if she likes it. It wasn't my favourite on the list. It smelt of boiled cabbage and disinfectant.

September 15th: I've found a writer's mentor on line.

September 17th: Alice doesn't like the home. No surprises there. But in the meantime I've found the most beautiful, wonderful home in Kingston. It's not far away. We go and have a look. I'd like to live there, it even has a cinema! We meet the staff. She likes it. We go back a few times. We have lunch there. She takes the medical and fills in all the forms. She said yes!

September 22nd: Got a five-page report on my book from the mentor I found and it's brilliant. Not because it says my book is fabulous, because it doesn't. It is telling me what it is and what it isn't and what I need to do. This is what I've been looking for. Now I have a 'To Do' list. She tells me I need to get a blog. What the heck is a blog?

September 25th: Everything is booked, the removal people are coming on Monday to move Alice into her new home. I get a call. She's changed her mind. OMG, I might swear! I can't believe it. So near and yet so far. It's a shame, but I understand. Change is difficult, especially when you're 93. I suppose we will muddle on a bit longer.

September 27th: I get a surge of energy and turn out my kitchen cupboards; it's always cathartic getting rid of the rubbish.

September 28th: Dad would have been 75 today.

October 2nd: Moved Connie to university.

October 5th: My friend Polly came round. She's going to help me make a blog. I need an elevator pitch too. Terminology. It's worse than technology!

November 4th: Just been to Rome with old friends. Not laughed so much in ages. We even danced in the street at 2am!

2016

January 4th: Everyone's back at school or university, and my blog is ready to go. Polly has done a fantastic job and I've done some drawings, simple and, even though I do say so myself, rather beautiful. Now I am ready to press send, yet something is stopping me. Should have gone into acting – the drama is Oscar-winning.

January 6th: Anyone would think I was launching Facebook. I'm so scared I ring my friend. 'Shall I do it? What if it's shit?' She tells me to get on with it, 'It's not as though you have any followers'. I laugh, and she's right. Nobody cares! I press send, my first post goes out, my Facebook friends 'like' it and I am happy. My blog is 'out there', *collectingconversations.com*. Five years from beginning to this point. I've even got myself a Twitter account!

January 28th: Met a woman at the gym, we get chatting. She's an art teacher. After a long conversation we make a plan to do swaps; I'll give her reflexology and she'll teach me art. Oh Lord, I can see where this is going. Maybe I've been suppressing an inner urge to be an artist after all!

January 31st: Terry Wogan died. Mum loved him. There's been a lot of death this year and it's only January.

February 9th: I've now been told more than three times that this project should be a play. It's a sign! Well, you know me, I love a sign and I'm always up for a challenge.

February 10th: Reasons why people work from their bed… I come downstairs, there's post to deal with, a couple of phone calls to be made, the washing to sort out, the dishwasher needs unloading and the fridge is empty. Distraction overload again.

April 3rd: My book isn't a book, it could be a play but, right now, it's not a book. I have a long list of interviews that might make for dialogue but not for page-turning. I'm having an arggghhh moment!

April 20th: Victoria Wood died. Mum loved her too. She got a mention in Mum's diaries: 'October 14th 2001: off to London to see Victoria Wood at the Albert Hall'.

May 3rd: Somethings happening. My period has gone and I seem to be having a 'welcome to the menopause' party. I'm having a taster session of every conceivable symptom there is, and it's all happening now!

May 30th: That was a month not to be repeated. I am definitely menopausal, and if this carries on, drugs will be needed.

June 1st: There's a playwriting course being advertised at The Clapham Omnibus, my local arts centre. I'll give them a ring. This had better not be another distraction.

June 7th: Just been to the course. That's what I needed, somewhere to be, homework to do and people to talk to. The only problem is, I don't have a play. I have a book, well, sort of.

June 14th: Slowly, slowly, part of my book is becoming a play. It's fun. They tell me I have a strong writing voice. I'll take anything I can get.

August 1st: I'm clearing out my wardrobe and I find Mum's box of diaries that I'd put there eight years ago. What I hadn't remembered was that I'd transferred the diaries into a new shoe box, the old one was falling apart. As I took the box from the shelf I was surprised and to be honest quite taken aback that I had unconsciously replaced the old shoe box with one from a shop called Fly. Their branding is an

enormous fly illustration right in the centre of the bright yellow box.

September 1st: That's a first. Normally by the end of the summer I'm at my wits' end, channeling my inner Garbo. But not this time. Maybe things are starting to change.

September 8th: Mum would have been 70 today.

September 13th: Veruccas are still not gone!

September 20th: The arts centre has asked me to tell a story. They have a night once a month called 'So, This Is What Happened…'. They want ordinary people to tell real stories about their life. We'll see!

September 21st: It's all kicking off with Alice again. She's been out for a walk and can't get back into her house. Her key won't work. Thankfully I have a spare. I let her back in but it's a struggle. The key doesn't seem to fit properly. She rings me 20 minutes later saying she now can't get out of her house. I go back. It's true, she's stuck. She can't open the door from the inside. I tell her she's going to have to have a new lock. We call a locksmith. He's there within the hour and thinks someone has tried to break in. On closer inspection, I think he's right. The door's been gouged with something. I ask Alice if anything's missing. She tells me she couldn't fathom why her jewellery box was on her bed, as she hadn't remembered putting it there. Oh, blimey. Here we go.

We call the police. She makes a statement but there's nothing they can do. Thankfully she's not too worried and she doesn't think anything is missing.

September 27th: Alice calls, 'Can you come round?' This time Alice has let someone into her house. A complete stranger came to her door giving her a sob story and managed to get herself into Alice's front room. Goodness knows how but, after about 15 minutes of careful negotiation, she manages to persuade the intruder to leave. Thankfully, once again, nothing was taken. We call the police, again. I am getting to see the reality of vulnerable, ageing people and it's not nice. Apart from the care system, which let's face it, doesn't exactly fill you with confidence, there's not a lot of help, apart from relying on neighbours. But I can't look after her 24/7 and anyway she'd hate it. I wish she'd gone in the home.

September 28th: Dad would have been 76 today. At last my book is starting to come together. I'm writing. I'm actually doing it!

October 6th: I'm on a roll. I am writing my story. There's some gaping holes that need filling but the baby is in the birth canal and she's coming out.

October 30th: Jheni unexpectedly came round. I hadn't seen her in eight months. I thought she'd vanished off the face of the earth. But right on cue, and coming full circle, she is now working with me on finally getting my project completed. I now know what structure is because I've got one and I'm writing everyday.

November 4th: Tonight I am telling my fly story. And I'm scared, but not as scared as I thought. Because I've practised. That in itself was possibly one of the most ridiculous things I've ever done. Every day this week, I stood in front of a mirror and recorded my talk. It was sooo embarrassing but funnily enough the more I did it the better it got. Funny that… practice something and you get better at it. Hallelujah!

November 5th: Last night's story went really well. There were about 80 people in the audience and, although I was a bit nervous, I was surprised at how calm I was. I got rapturous applause and even some laughs. Will you look at me!

December 18th: I've been too busy writing to mark everything down in my diary but as Christmas approaches, I am slowing down ready for the inevitable break.

December 27th: Carrie Fisher died, and George Michael on Christmas Day. What is going on? It's been a year of many deaths; nine of my friends lost their Mum this year too.

December 28th: I'm sat here getting my book ready for its final edit. It's 4.30 in the afternoon, and I've just realised that it was nine years ago today that my mum died. Every year since, I have posted a comment on Facebook acknowledging it. But not today; I forgot! That, in itself, is a sure sign that I am ready to move on.

December 29th: I've just read somewhere that having a project makes you focused, and that makes for a more rounded person. Not sure I need any more rounding – 107 interviews, cakes, chocolate and lunches have rounded me so well I have put on two stone. Oops! That's next year's project!

December 30th: I've popped in to see Alice. She's doing fine, not much has changed. She's lonely, but she manages. I think there's a lesson here for us all, keep changing and adapting or we might eventually be so scared of change that, when we need it most, we won't be able to accept it. On a positive note, the veruccas have gone and I'm now channelling my inner Picasso regularly.

December 31st: The last day of 2016. I'm finally finishing my project. I'm setting it free and will bask for a while in the knowledge that I did it. I actually did it. It took such a long time but I did it!

I've just told Martin I've finished. I think he's very pleased. It's been nearly as painful for him as it has me. He's just asked me how I feel. Gosh, I'm feeling a bit emotional. I didn't expect that. I thought I would be relieved to the point of bursting but, no, I feel a bit sad. And the tiniest bit proud that I'VE DONE IT!

✳

December 2017: A year on since I finished writing and I had no idea there would be so much more to do: rewrites, edits, proofing and the whole production of getting it into an actual book; something I was totally clueless about. As fate would have it, I was at the bus stop chatting to a neighbour I've known for 20 years, when for some reason I asked him 'What is it you actually do, I've never asked you?', 'I print books - done it for 44 years, I know everything there is to know about printing, you need a book printing, I'm your man!'

Tomorrow he's sending my book to China where it will get the 5 star treatment and all I have to do is hope and pray I've not made any mistakes and I can sell the 1,000 copies I've ordered.

I did in fact sell-out and you now have in your hand a copy from the second print run - I can't quite believe how well it's going.

Part Two
The Questions

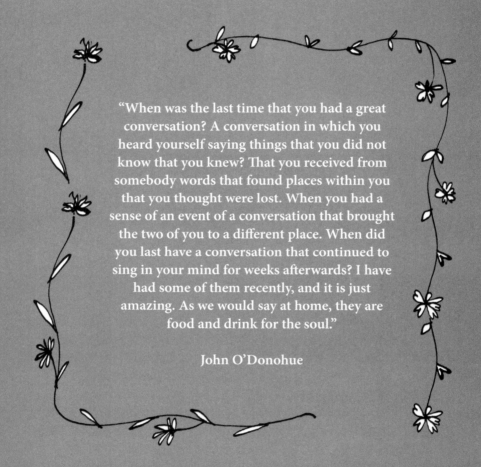

"When was the last time that you had a great conversation? A conversation in which you heard yourself saying things that you did not know that you knew? That you received from somebody words that found places within you that you thought were lost. When you had a sense of an event of a conversation that brought the two of you to a different place. When did you last have a conversation that continued to sing in your mind for weeks afterwards? I have had some of them recently, and it is just amazing. As we would say at home, they are food and drink for the soul."

John O'Donohue

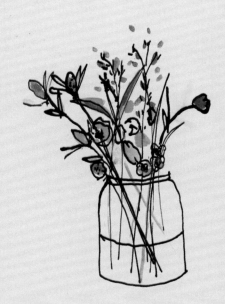

What I did…

Welcome to the wonderful world of women – their answers to my questions. I started out with women close to home as I still had the school run to do. But, as time went on, I travelled up and down the country too: back to my roots to see women who had been in my childhood and old friends of my Mum's. I didn't purposely seek out women to make sure I'd ticked all the demographic boxes but, as my project evolved, a wider spread of women developed. I asked childhood friends, teachers, old employers and shopkeepers, former colleagues, clients, neighbours and mums at the school gate. New friends and old, from all backgrounds and cultures. Women who are lifetime friends and those who became fleeting guests.

These women are a cross-section of society from all over the world. Some are married; some aren't, some are white; some aren't, some are gay; some aren't, some are single; some aren't, some have children; some don't. Some this, some that. I don't like box-ticking. For me, women are women, their age and experiences may differ, as do their personalities, but the labels we put on people are just that: labels. It's actually refreshing to read the answers alone, without any back story. As Jayne said in her foreward 'These sentences open those everyday worlds of emotion and struggle – worlds that are familiar and alien to us and worlds we might be frightened of. These short sentences are how stories work – we are invited to fill in the gaps, flesh things out with our imagination, to reflect on our own lives: we are transported into life itself by what may look like a mundane comment'. So please take your time to ponder the mundane.

For this part of the book, I'm not giving you details or demographics about the women. If you'd like to read more about each interview and the person behind the comments, have a look at my blog *collectingconversations.com*. Most of their names are changed for confidentiality.

Each person I interviewed either came to my house or I went to theirs. My plan was to make a day of it and if we didn't finish, we'd make another date. I made a lot of lunches; not a drop of alcohol was drunk but we did get through an awful lot of chocolate to satisfy the afternoon slump (there's something in that SNAP sound I never tire of hearing.) It's no coincidence that there is a whole page dedicated to how we feel about chocolate later on.

I didn't specifically ask these women to tell me their life stories but, inevitably, once you get talking, flow happens. These snapshots highlight the stark reality of how we duck and dive though the passage of time.

With over 2,000 answers, I didn't have the room to put every single one down so I've chosen commentary that reflects the essence of our experiences. It was whilst editing, I realised the potency in these pearls of insight. There was something about seeing everything come together that drew me to the conclusion that we really are a wonderful community and I just wish the media and aspects of our society would stop telling us any different.

There's some housekeeping:

In case you're wondering – I didn't ask about sex. To be honest I hadn't even thought about it. A couple of women mentioned it and what they said was funny, 'I once had a desire to sit on one of those huge cream cakes from Patisserie Valerie, so I did and had it licked off me' and 'Do you think it's acceptable for me to steal the batteries from the kids' Darth Vader to put in my vibrator?' but that's all folks – no more sex from here on in.

The answers are in chronological age groups starting with the thirty -somethings right through to the ninety-somethings. At the bottom of each page you'll find more extracts from Mum's diaries. I wanted her to be part of this book too. Where I can I've tried to put them under relevant topics. Where I can't they're just random.

There are 18 questions in total. The chapter title is the question I asked. Five of the questions provoked single word answers, so I've chosen to make them into

my own word clouds, highlighting the top four words that were said most often. Please feel free to underline, circle and graffiti the pages as much as you like.

During the course of our conversations, other subjects would come up. It became apparent there was much more to say. It's easy with hindsight that maybe I should have asked more questions, but my project was already big enough and sometimes you've just got to stop, but if there was time at the end of our chats, I would fire out a few more questions on topics that kept coming up like chocolate, shoes and household chores. As these subjects are very much part of our everyday lives, I wanted to include them. You'll also find the occasional double spread of comments interspersed between the questions.

If you would like to, I would love you to be part of this project by answering the questions too. There's space on most pages for you to write your thoughts. Take your time, don't rush. It might take a few hours or even a few days. Find some time just for you or maybe get a friend to ask you the questions, even record your answers. You'll probably get quite a lot of insight especially when you hear your own thoughts out loud.

As you can imagine, I know these words pretty well by now but I still get fresh insight each time I re-read them. May I suggest once you've finished reading that you go back from time to time and revisit them. You'll be surprised how these comments impact on you time and time again, and if you have answered the questions, it will be interesting to see how your own thoughts have evolved over time.

Question 1

How are you?

I've often watched people when they start a conversation with, 'Hi, how are you?', and the usual automatic response is, 'Fine thanks, and you?' I know we can't spend hours in the supermarket queue waiting to hear how someone actually is, but I'd often wonder, 'What would they really like to say?' Now I had the time, I thought I'd ask.

This was my opener, and, often from habit, they would say 'fine' but I'd pause and ask again, 'How are you, really?' This was the opportunity to go with the flow. This question took the longest to answer. We would meander along the pathways of their lives not knowing where we'd end up.

People are fascinating and you have absolutely no idea what's going to come out of their mouths. Most surprising and it happened several times, was the women's own shock about what they had said: 'I had no idea that was an issue', or 'Oh my God, I can't believe I'm crying already'. It shows how much we bottle stuff up. We often ignore things that are going on in our minds, not giving ourselves time to digest our thoughts. It became apparent we need to share more.

I asked this question because I am genuinely interested to know what's going on, on the inside. I'm not keen on the superficiality of general conversation. I am intrigued and fascinated by people and always surprised and delighted once the veil comes off.

I love the openness and honesty in these answers. I've asked this question over 100 times and it's true, we do seem to mellow with time.

Here are their responses...

The 30s

I'm not married, I don't have any kids and I have weight issues. But, on the positive side, I have a boyfriend and I have just got myself a new job.

Another decade begins. I'm not feeling great, I'm a bit fed up. Not for any particular reason, I'm just not my usual self. I'm normally quite positive, but not necessarily about myself. It's difficult to hear my own advice.

I am exhausted and sleeping a lot. No matter how much I sleep, I need more. I have aches and pains all over my body at the moment and I'm getting my periods quite a lot, which I shouldn't be, 'cos I'm on the pill. I bleed all the time. I've had a mental and emotional breakdown and I don't know what to do. I show the world one thing but, deep down there's a whole other side, and it's scary.

I'm feeling OK. I can let things go now, I am more accepting. I am feeling more serene and am learning not to get so angry and pissed off at things.

I'm definitely on a journey. I wish I was at the end of it sometimes. It's uncomfortable and traumatic at times. Life is tough, it's a part of growing up. My life's a lot less hard than 99% of the world's population. I have so much. There's a part of me that still wants my mum to come and make it all better.

I'm fine, I thought I would be happier. I'm happy in myself, but I would like to have a husband and be married. It would be nice if someone was there for me.

I don't know how I am.

The 40s

We might move house. I'm in the middle of lots of decisions. I'm teetering on the edge a bit and I'm not sure what's going to happen. The day-to-day is fine, but there's a lot going on behind the scenes. This morning I sat on the floor in my laundry room and cried.

I'm in a happy, reflective place, settled. I'm having lots of memories, lots of things that have been swallowed up are coming up to the surface. There have been lots of fears and anxieties about the future but I've survived and it's not traumatic.

I'm feeling happy and relaxed in this moment right now. I am looking forward to my day. On a deeper level, I'm a bit confused: uncertain of my future, my career and where I'm going to live. I feel changes are afoot. I'm going with the flow and allowing myself to be open, not worried, just uncertain.

My love life is disappointing and I keep asking, 'Why me?' But equally, I feel let down by others. I'm sick of making the same mistakes.

At this very point in time, I have a decrepit uncle staying. We pass him around to where the music stops. It's 'unwanted relative syndrome' and it causes many arguments with my siblings.

I am tired, a lot! My periods are heavier than they used to be. I need to claim back a bit of 'me' time. I'm trying to get fit. There's a realisation, if I don't get fit, that I've allowed life to take over. I don't think I've ever made a firm decision about anything. I've just gone on to the next thing. In lots of ways I am happier than I've been before. I don't have the 'I should have said that' anymore and, actually, people like me for who I am.

I'm at a crossroads. I am waiting to sign divorce papers and am hugely fearful as to what's out there. I could have him back or I could be free. Do I have the strength enough to make changes for the better? I accept full responsibility for my part in this.

Right now, I am feeling good. But I am worried: since the birth of my second child I have stress incontinence. Wee slowly drips out of me as I walk up the stairs. I have to wear a pad. Should get it sorted now? I worry about what it will be like when I am older.

I am a middle-aged woman, mother of two, wife, home-keeper, performance management consultant, and knackered. My looks are going, my health is deteriorating, my hearing's got worse, my bum is lower than it used to be and wrinkles are appearing. Most days I do look at my life and appreciate it. I'm a long way on my journey, I can look back and see how things have shaped me. I can see what life's all about at this stage and it's no fucking picnic; it's an endurance test. Some days are fantastic. I look at other people's lives and I think 'Thank God for my life', but things can change so quickly.

I'm optimistic. I'm always challenging something. I am incapable of not challenging the supermarket shopping list. It doesn't matter what it is, everything gets interrogation. There's routine and structure to anchor me – it drives my husband mad. There's a strong backbone to the way I live. But I do try and stop and make time for myself.

I'm not happy, I'm bored! I'm trying to figure out what I can be when I grow up. I love my daughter and being a mum but I'm just not where I expected. You're trapped by the decisions you make. I'd like to be working, more financially independent. Part of the problem with being a stay-at-home mum is your confidence gets knocked.

I'm muddled and confused, it's not the best time of my life.
I don't want to feel like this much longer.

I am fucked up and severely struggling. I don't think it's an age thing, I don't think it's a mid-life crisis. I don't know where I am going.

I'm in a good place. At a time in my life where I'm very grateful and appreciate my life, after a long period of stress and struggling. I am actually in love with my husband and gratitude is huge in my life at the moment. I found it very difficult to let go of things but I'm not a hoarder anymore. You can only be responsible for yourself, don't try and take responsibility for others.

I am beginning to feel invisible and I bloody well don't like it! If I was married I'd probably feel different about it. I know I still have something to offer but externally there's a flaw in me. I wonder if I will ever have a relationship again.

My knee-jerk reaction to this question is to say
'I am fine', even though it's not necessarily so.

I feel contented, I feel like I'm at the end part of a journey with fresh new horizons. I'm more me than I've ever been. I've let the mantles of confusion and self-doubt go. I've done it by being incredibly unhappy and realising it is just in my head and it's a self-indulgence. It's been a gradual process. I read a lot, which has helped. I'm fearlessly facing myself with forgiveness, appreciating the here and now. I'm looking forward and genuinely letting go of the past. I see the past as a process of how it has brought me to where I am now. I'm grateful for the difficult times and experiences I've gone through – 'growing pains'. By looking back, I can appreciate who I am now.

I am up and down, the high is very high and I am happy to be alive,
but the low is exhausting and I am very lonely inside.

I am noticing the wrinkles more and it's not good. I am marginally depressed by it! It's a fact of life and you just have to get on with it. I am 50 soon, it's a marker in life, another box on the form you fill in. I don't remember my 40s. I do feel middle-aged, especially when I am with younger people. There are things I wish I'd wanted to do when I was younger, like having a threesome! It had been a passing thought that had occurred to me but the opportunity never arose.

I am at a crossroads because of my age. I'm still renting and constantly worrying about money. If I was two years younger I wouldn't be thinking about it. I am happy in my career but I worry about the future.

The 50s

I am a lot better than at 30, although there's a looming anxiety about my mother and what I should do with her.

The other day I fell over, it bruised my dignity. I thought, 'Is this it, is this the start of becoming physically decrepit?'

Really good, never felt better. My 50th birthday party was a turning point, a watershed, a coming out: 50 and proud. A liberation.

I am at a hiatus in my life… What to do next? I look back, a third has been up to university, a third has been working and a third bringing up kids. There's a gap in my life at the moment and it's affected my confidence.

I am knackered. I worked last night and am working again today, there's a lot going on. I am a nurse in A&E. Work knackers me so much more now. It's more the psychological and emotional consequences; the more senior you are the more responsibility you have. The process has changed a lot since I started. We are much more answerable to things.

Children can make you feel worthless: 'Mum, at home all day'. I am trying to work out what to do. I am quite good at knowing what I don't want. One thing's for sure, I need human interaction and it's good to get out.

I don't feel 100%. I feel my medication doesn't agree with me, I'd like to come off it.

I long to be free. If it was me, only me, I wouldn't be here in England. We live in matchboxes. Humans need space. I just need to be where I can be free. I am free-spirited. Here in London, we are all rushing.

It's not the most smooth-running period of my life, we've had two deaths and a break-in. There is something changing in my universe. There's quite a lot of poorly people in my life at the moment, and it brings it home.

I'm in a transitional phase. I am working less hours and now based at home. I am in much more control. I have time on my hands which is quite curious but enjoyable. I am practising music after a long time. Being ill brought it to a head. I physically couldn't have carried on. It was a cumulative effect, I had been thinking for a few years about taking time off but couldn't see a way out. It's been very liberating. Sometimes I reflect and feel a sense of deep relief. I thought I'd miss the social side but I don't. I don't miss the endless bollocks.

My body is starting to fall apart, it's making me aware of the ageing process. I have ageing parents and they are shrinking and disappearing from the world. There is an end. What is the path to the end? I'm not in control of it and it's scary. Time's running out. Am I really using every day I have as well as I should? Life's a bit mundane, there's not a lot to it. We are living normal, repetitive lives. I am coming to terms with that. I thought I'd have more of a 'Wow-ee!' sort of life. It's not going to change. I am focusing on the small things, mini-goals, like putting in a new Venetian blind; it can make all the difference! I want to feel content within myself. I am very good at talking myself down.

There has been a shift this year. I am moving in the right direction.
I have a great life ahead of me.

It's a beautiful day and I am feeling good. I am content,
but it doesn't mean there aren't any problems, but life is good.

My Mum isn't well. To see her is very important.

Life is getting harder on every level. Since 50 I've really noticed ageing and its difficulties. I look at myself in the mirror and go, 'Shit, a woman in her 50s!'

I am using this year to face up to the next age group by changing things and doing things that I haven't done before. I am trying to look for a different direction.

I am physically tired but peaceful inside.

The other day I had an epiphany – life is a privilege, it's a gift, take a proper look.

I know there's always something, a drama in life. There's no point feeding it. I don't react to things, I just breathe and let it happen. I go quiet and inside myself. Often the moment passes and if it doesn't I can detach myself. Even with my own family I can detach. It's other peoples energy that affects me, not my own. I am quite a contented person.

The 60s

I am healthier than I have ever been. I've worked myself into the ground for the past 27 years and most recently had been a headmistress in a school abroad and, now I've stopped, it's the best thing that's ever happened.

I'm a little pissed off; I miss my kids. My kids were my life but now they've moved out. I worry if me and my husband will get back to the way we were before kids. I'm in limbo, I'm making more time to catch up with friends.

I am doing a course and I love it. I love learning, why should you stop just because you're 60?

I am fine, I am glad to say. People often at my age are on tablets and none of the unpleasant diseases of old age have got to me yet. I am determined to pack in as much as possible before I get to 90. I have terrific freedom.

Absolutely brilliant, having retired. An overriding feeling of 'What can I do next?'. I've run a shop for over 25 years and now I'm finally getting to see who I really am, without the scaffolding. I am in a reflective phase, which I am finding really, really good. I am helping five-year-olds read one day a week at a local school, and spending time listening to an elderly man of 82 through Age Concern another day a week. I can do whatever I want with my life, it's very freeing, there are no rules. I don't ever go down the 'I wish…' route, things happen at the right time. Listen to your feminine instinct.

Life is good. My attitude is 'Stuff it'. I don't worry about anything. As long as I can get away and do my own thing.

I am happy in life. I've always been positive and calm. I don't get stressed, there's no point.

The 70s

I am very good and content, even happy. I am very good at putting things to the back of my mind, like bad memories and bad stuff. Commitment is the thing. I've never wanted more than I've had. We are comfortable, we've had the same home, same friends and family in and out of our home for the last 50 years.

I am really comfortable with my life. I am very happy with my kids and my grandchildren. I have a good relationship with my husband.

I've just had a new knee and it's very painful. Because of this I am feeling old before my time. My husband died four years ago; I miss him terribly, but otherwise I am very happy.

They say it gets easier the older you get but I don't think so. Since my husband has died I am jealous. I am jealous of friends that go away on holiday and go out in the evenings. I am on my own.

I am very happy, more than I've ever been.

I have up days and down days – I am a cheerful optimist.

The 80s

I have always been contented with my lot. Accepting, always accepting and grateful for what I've got. I don't have much but I appreciate things. All my family are well off. I don't envy them, I've never been jealous of others. If I need something I will work for it and go and buy it.

I am very happy. I am acclimatising to a small situation.
I've just moved here from my large family house.

I have no initiative and I berate myself for that. I am quite happy but I don't like being old. Since I was 80, I have moved house and I love it. It's the physicality of getting old: I'm not strong in my body and it makes me so cross. Not to be able to do the things I used to do. I think it's important to keep busy and your mind active.

Some days I have more energy than others.
Sometimes being with other people overwhelms me. I like my own space.

The 90s

Inside I feel 16. I am the same sort of person I always was but now
I'm more patient. My dread is dementia.

I am just back from Trinidad. We had six weeks there. I travel a lot.
Two years ago, I walked the Great Wall of China!

Since the pensioners' club closed life's a bit boring now and I don't go anywhere.
It's put paid to my sanity. I've been inside now for nearly a year. I have very bad
rheumatoid arthritis and am housebound. It's knocked my confidence and my
body has suffered too. I am now only seven stone.

So how are you, really?

September 8th 2004 Sad, deflated and vulnerable

Question 2

How do you see yourself?

Who is it looking back at you when you look in the mirror? Do you like what you see? I meant metaphorically but for many of the women sat in front of me they took it literally and immediately went into habitual self-sabotaging negatives about how much they hate their bodies.

Body image wasn't something I wanted to cover. It's not a topic where we naturally shine, but now I'd asked the question it was hard to steer away from the negativity. I think we feel quite comfortable with our own self-doubt; it slips off the tongue nicely. But thankfully it seems we care less and less as we age.

I rephrased my question and asked, 'How do you see yourself inside and out?'

Here are their responses...

The 30s

I'm very hard on myself and I always have been. If I can't do my best, then I have failed. It's so easy to be positive to others but not to myself.

When I was 13 I got a lead part in a play. There were two leads. The other girl was very thin, so I starved myself.

Unforgiving, and I hold a grudge.

Every day I wake up and think how fat or thin I am.

Confident and strong. I'm just getting on with life. I'm proactive, I make things happen. I'm not someone who sits back and waits for things to happen. I don't credit myself for what I do. I'm driven and focused. If there is no goal I'm all over the place.

I'd like not to give a shit, but I am totally taken in by it all.
I want to be thinner, toned and tanned.

I'm not honest enough, I say the things people want to hear. When I'm down, I'm down but when I'm up, I'm slightly over-talkative. I am hypersensitive to other people's feelings.

I find it hard to praise myself physically.

For a long time I saw myself as not good enough and, on a bad day, I can go down that path. There's a spark that's beginning to think, 'On whose say?'

The 40s

There is a dichotomy; on one level I think I'm solid, capable, a good provider, ticking all the boxes and, on the other hand, I am very insecure and I think I'll get found out.

I have no body issues, I like the way I look.

I am very critical of myself. I have low self-esteem and I feel I'm not good enough. I have a fear of failure, I worry about getting it right.

I like my new boobs. No-one loves them more than me.

When I am drunk I see myself as really hot.

I don't like my body, well the bottom half. It makes me sad that I can't strip off. I am very body conscious.

I sometimes wake up in the morning, look in the mirror and go… 'Is that me?'

Judgmental.

I like being naked and I like my feet, my hands and my breasts. My ambition is to grow to love my saddle-bags, because I love everything else.

I am constantly trying to do things to make me feel better about myself.

There's a tiny bit of me that wants to let it all go and say 'fuck it', but it's a struggle for me as I am vain.

I always regret not liking me in the now. I am trying to be more like that now as opposed to, 'My life will get better when…'.

If I were a dog I'd be a poodle. I have fine ankles and wrists and
a fluffy bit in the middle!

Struggling, in deep water and out of control.

Confident, positive, enthusiastic, grounded, and a little lost. Lacking a bit of
focus, but I'm feeling empowered.

As I get older, I'm more forgiving. Young women should enjoy their natural
youthfulness and leave the handbags until they're older and need the props.

I wish I was more laid back. I have a big ugly tummy and wrinkles on my
beautiful face. I'm partially deaf, with a dodgy hip and knee. I allow myself to
get too stressed.

A positive person with a calming influence.

I'm a bit delusional about my size. I think I am a size 12 but I'm not. I wear
Demis Roussos clothing. I feel deflated. I grab food and comfort eat. I probably
think about my size all day long. I would be upset if someone said something.
One day someone at the office did say something and in his honesty it cut me
down and I was very upset. It hit a nerve and my self-destruct button came on.

I have a good heart and I've got great legs.

I don't find myself attractive. I see myself as an irritating buzzy fly.

I have skinny wrists and a longish neck. I look like a giraffe.
Then there's this body: I could do without the body.

My boobs are so big and I'm so short that they get stuck under door handles
when I walk past!

March 20th 1997 **Cholesterol test clear**

As a scrumpled up bit of paper on the floor, downtrodden. I am going through a nasty divorce. But I know it's only for now.

Being small in a tall world. I'm not very attractive. I am small and dumpy. I don't like much about myself. Sometimes I don't think I am a very nice person. I can be abrasive. I lose my temper quickly. I am selfish, I know what I want so I override other people. I don't suffer fools and I'm quite irritable.

I don't hate myself, I just don't like the way I look. If I could I'd change myself physically, but am happy on the inside.

As a vibrant force of life. Energetic, enthusiastic with fucking bells on, to the point when I could slap myself sometimes. I love the fact I can say no.

You should be comfortable in your own body but I am not 99% of the time. If only I could practise what I preach.

Although I get tearful, I'm actually a lot stronger than I think I am.

I have broad shoulders, I think that's metaphorical.

Somebody who's not terribly exciting. I'm never going to set the world on fire but I'm never going to fuck it up either. I'm always striving to do a little bit better; it does bother me that I always want to do better.

I see my bum dimples and I am horrified by them.

A work in progress, different on different days. On a tightrope between mental illness and a strong coper.

I'm not really good at being 100% myself in other people's company. If people saw me for who I am, they might not like me and judge me.

I now like my body for the first time. I like my teeth for the first time, and I like having grey hair too. By repairing my physical body, it has given me confidence and an appreciation of myself that I didn't have before. I used to feel vaguely agoraphobic going out because I felt fat. There were old voices in my head telling me I was unattractive. I was often put down physically. Now I can accept myself. I can like and love myself. There's a lot of ego and not a lot of confidence. If you're not happy with your body, there's no quick fix, just loving hard work and a re-education of how to eat and move.

I see myself as a middle-aged woman with unfulfilled interests.

You have to be happy with your body because it gives you confidence. It doesn't matter what shape you are just don't make it a big issue of it. Don't become obsessed with the way you look.

I'm outwardly scary and strong but inwardly fragile, intolerant and half-full.

I like my strong thighs.

Broken, a mess, happy, content, a bit screwed up.

Fat and old.

I like myself, I didn't in my early 20s, but I do now.

I used to worry what people thought of me but now I'm more confident. I'm older and wiser.

It depends on the day and which mirror I am looking in. I let age bother me too much. If I look and think about it for too long I can get downhearted.

I see myself attracted to broken things and then try to mend them.

Because I'm used to struggling, it's become the norm, it's a badge of capability. I can't ask for help.

Fear of not being good enough. Lack of confidence, lack of voice, indecisive but deep down I know exactly what I want. I am gullible, passive, someone who's a little awkward in their own skin.

I like people but I need my own space. I must learn not to be so bossy, which is fucking difficult for Taureans, as we are a pain in the arse.

Somebody who is trying to evolve. Hopefully open to change. I'm more afraid of my mum not changing than me.

Typically mediocre, it's always fairly irritated me. I'm not really good at anything. I really did think I would set the world alight but I didn't put in the effort.

I move with my heart. I'm a person with integrity. I'm happy with what I've done.

I can't say no, I bend over backwards for everyone outside the home. I can't be nasty. I always think about others and not for myself. I definitely have the Catholic guilt, my mother and aunt are servants to the world.

Increasingly like my mother!

I've led a truthful life and it's been hard along the way. I have to keep recalibrating what have I learnt and what's changed; I am very reflective.

As things go I am OK. I am a positive person, when I don't like something I change it. I am an altruistic person, kind and probably a pain in the arse. I'm very relaxed. It gives me pleasure to touch nice things. I am sensual, life is about guilty pleasures.

I'm not two-faced. If I don't like you I avoid you; what you see is what you get!

Intelligent, but never did anything to reach my full potential. I'm not ambitious enough to go for the things I wanted to go for. I am apathetic and opinionated to a fault. I have a temper. I'm loyal and a happy person. I feel a tremendous amount of responsibility and guilt. I am a friend you can count on.

I have an inner core of strength because I have come through some really tricky times.

A person who has a lot going on in her head. I am quite at peace being on my own.

The 50s

My outlook on life is younger than I am. I never see myself as 50!

Most of my life I have hated my body. I grew up thinking I had the fattest thighs. No one ever told me I looked nice.

Big, strong, fierce: a wild horse that's actually quite timid.

Quite a 'plain Jane' with bleached hair. I won't speak up even though I know I'm right. I keep the peace.

Slightly in limbo, the kids are away at uni and I have an ageing mum.

I am much happier now. I live in my body now where I didn't use to. I'm proud of it.

I am very comfortable with my physical appearance but I'm not necessarily comfortable in my head.

At 24 I had a breast reduction. I was a different person afterwards, more confident.

I've reached an accommodation about who I am.

I don't like what I look like in the mirror but I'm too lazy to do anything about it. I could go on a diet but I just buy bigger clothes instead. I have more to worry about than getting into a size 12. If my health suffered then I would.

I see myself as a crap mother, I look at other people and think they've done it far better than me.

I still have that 'I've got to…' high expectation. I am becoming more mindful of what I want to do rather than what I ought to do.

I see myself as a good person, I always see the positive in people. I don't think anyone is a lower person than me. In quite a dull way, I want to be nice and kind. I'm not a 'zippity-do-dah' sort of person but I'm a nice person. I am pleased that I'm not bothered about what people think of me. I used to be caught up in caring about what other people thought, but not now.

I am a reasonably well-functioning person. I don't have too many mental health issues. I don't feel dissatisfied, I am mostly content with my lot.

I am an ordinary person, and I like that.

Kindness can be mistaken for a pushover. Sometimes I am a pushover because I haven't got the time to argue.

Creative, organised, even funny. My kids like my company, which is nice because I didn't like my mum's company.

Confident, serene, happy and beautiful.

It varies. Confident me is outgoing, I can do anything, I am fully content as long as I'm busy. Then I have these pockets of self-doubt and self-loathing, they are fairly fleeting and they will be over something specific.

April 15th 2000 **No change at the hospital but they want me to have a mastectomy!**

I see myself as a less secure person than a lot of people see me. They see the veneer as more competent and capable than I really am. I do see myself as fortunate though and lucky to have my life.

I love being in a supportive role; I'm not a leader. I am a giver and it can be quite damaging. It's not very healthy to give too much, I need to take every now and then.

The 60s

I worry more than I used to.

Personally, I am not happy with my body, but it serves me very well.

I am inspirational, with a lazy streak. Versatile, independent, practical, matter of fact, earthy, caring, motherly, home-loving, adventurous, sensitive, intelligent, God-loving, creative… This statement was done under duress because I don't like self-praise.

Beauty is in the eyes of the people you associate with around the same age.

I am good at supporting people emotionally. I am a good listener and I don't need to impose my views.

I used to be very conscious of my tummy, but now
I don't worry and it's very liberating.

I'd like to be thin, who wouldn't?
How fat or thin has affected whether I have gone out or not.

I'm quite a slob really. I don't like getting up, I have a long list of 'to dos'.

I don't think too much, that's how I get through. I focus on what I have to do and hope I get it done in the day. If I do that, then I am quite happy with myself. I used to stay up 'til two in the morning cleaning my cupboards, I don't do that anymore.

I don't care. I wear what I want, go where I want and eat what I want.

I'm too old to care.

As a little elderly lady. I like that as I can listen into conversations on the tube. I always dress down, I don't want to attract attention. I like to observe and watch the world go by. I don't see myself as anything special.

I see myself as getting older and not being able to do the things I want to do. I don't want to be a burden, and it worries me because my dad's got dementia.

I've got great boobs!

I am irritatingly open. I think a little bit of mystery in a woman is a good thing. I think, 'Today I will sit there and be passive' - but I never am.

Half of me is great and half of me is a fucking bore.

I am absolutely not happy and I need to lose weight. I used to buy clothes that were too small for me and I'd burst out of them.

I look in the mirror, and my mother is staring back at me. I see her mannerisms, my voice has plummeted. I am completely happy in myself, right or wrong.

I am quite happy with my size, I've passed 50, so who cares?

I've made a conscious effort to start looking people in the eye. It was an observation someone once made – "look at people when you talk to them".

I like to chill out, but I do feel guilty that I 'should' be doing things,
but I like chillin' best.

The 70s

I've always been very conscious of being too fat. I was as greedy then, as I am
now. I used to be called 'Fatty Ed.' I was given amphetamines when I was 14.
The weight just fell off but after the 'high' came the 'low'. I had to be weaned off
them because they became illegal.

I think you fundamentally stay the same, sometimes you surprise yourself. It's
tempting to accept things as they are. I was much more confident before I got
married; socially he was the more confident one and I became his appendage.
Now I'm on my own; I'm being more open in what I say and I'm a bit more
confident too. He'd like routine whereas I can do without it.

I think I'm pretty damn good for 70!

Possibly too critical a nature. I can see bad where my husband can see good.
I am picky to a ridiculous degree.

I'm a bit too willing. I'm afraid of confrontation, I shy away from problems. I'm
a bit of an act sometimes. I'm a pleaser, I say yes when I mean no.

I have a lot of energy but it just doesn't go on as long so I have a rest during the
day then I can go out in the evening.

I think I look tired and washed out without make-up. I want to make the best
of what I've got. The ageing process isn't much fun. I think people who have
Botox take something away from their character.

The 80s

I don't have any hang-ups about people, I take everyone on face value. I care about suffering and people's plights. I am a lot about animals. I became a vegetarian at six years old. I was evacuated to Wales during the war; when I saw the sheep in the fields I decided there and then I wasn't going to eat meat anymore.

I remember being very plump as a teenager, but I soon lost it all when the boys started looking.

I have been driven mad by my mind. I feel too much and see too much.

There are two sides to me; one side is very serious, emotional and sentimental then the other is waspish, never wanting to grow old. I have always been perceptive and psychic. I get premonitions.

Somebody who had a good education thrust upon her. I wouldn't never have dreamt of saying no because of my strict upbringing.

I am satisfied with myself. I don't want anything to change. In spite of everything life hasn't been, I've never been short of money or hungry. I have a happy marriage.

I have no initiative and I berate myself for that. At times, I'm not a very nice person, I can be catty. I like to think I can keep a secret but once or twice I've let it slip out, it caused amazing consequences.

I try to be friendly, I didn't used to be. I was shy, I like to be thought well of. I do care what other people think.

As an elderly lady, I'm quite ordinary.

The 90s

I am self-satisfied, I have no regrets. All that I've gone through is what should have happened, it's what is written in the stars. I am Hindu, and in our culture when a child is born their future is read. No matter how you try to avoid it, it will happen.

I am a listener and an observer, then a talker. I am not quick to pass judgement.

I am happy in my skin; you have to love yourself. I've always loved myself. I have never felt dissatisfied about myself. Life wasn't always easy but I took it in my stride. I don't dwell on it, I just get on with it.

Go on, have a look, what do you see?

Question 3

How do you think other people see you?

Honestly? I would have liked this page to be blank. Why should we care what other people think of us? But most of us do. There's an inherent desire to belong and to be accepted.

I found that some women wanted to be seen by the image they portrayed and didn't want to show the world the 'real' them. I wondered if this front could create a barrier that allows no-one in, or the real person out?

Thankfully, most of the responses were positive and strong. I was surprised to see, especially as we are quick to put ourselves down, that in the eyes of other people, we see ourselves as strong, caring, confident and kind.

Here are their responses...

Caring Encouraging Funny Independent Trustworthy Neurotic Attractive

Eccentric Wise Creative Different

Approachable Bossy Highly emotional Sorted Brave Impulsive Warm Friendly

Happy Non conforming Quirky Uptight Vulgar Generous spirited Impatient Unshockable

Reliable Fun Confident Vulnerable Childish Outgoing Reserved Stylish Worrier Right Kind

Boring Shy Listener **I don't care what people think** Capable Quiet Organised Energetic

Compensating Frivolous Open Scary Giving Sensitive Sociable Calm Talkative

Soft Positive Hard Miserable Opinionated Pushover Empathetic Busy

Confident Chaotic Aloof Loyal Standoffish High achieving Strong

Content Uptight Silly Intimidating Passionate Ugly Enthusiastic Late

Forgetful Insecure Moody Stressed Arrogant Clumsy Threatening Single minded......

What would you say? _____

January 2nd 2002 **Taught Amy to make flapjack**

91

Question 4

What do you like about yourself?

What do we like about being us? After a little too much self-sabotage in previous answers I wanted to draw out some positives. Trickier than I'd hoped! Once again most started off with 'Well, I know what I don't like…' Just so you know, the work behind getting the good stuff was no mean feat. The return to negativity was persistent. But I was insistent that this chapter is only about the good stuff.

It's an awkward question I know but, for once, I wanted the women in front of me to spend a few moments appreciating themselves.

Here are their responses…

The 30s

Saying good things about myself doesn't feel too good (*not a good start!*)

I like that I am on a journey. For a long time it burdened me, now I realise you never get there.

**I try really hard to be kind and treat people the way I like to be treated.
I love my sense of humour.**

I do the best with my capabilities. I try to understand myself and other people. I think I do things just well enough.

I like me, no-one can be me. I feel I am different and I was put here to make a difference. I'm like an agony aunt, it gives me great honour. It makes me feel good that people tell me stuff.

The 40s

**I enjoy learning about myself. You should always explore and visit things…
Let's go to the dark places.**

I'm honest and kind. I am mindful. I try. I'm loving and giving.

I am very open and people can talk to me. I like that I keep in touch with people. I put effort into friendships. I am confident, caring, kind, passionate and enthusiastic. I have a good sense of humour and lots of energy.

The overall package is alright. I have good energy and I like that. I like that I can get on with people from all walks of life.

That I can let go and enjoy myself. I am expressive and I love dancing. I am caring and independent. Although I might not have a lot, what I've got is mine. I'm really settled now and contented.

I like me a lot.

I like me as Mummy. I like my kids and I am proud of them. I like the fact that I am hardworking, kind, committed. I am driven by my passions.

I can't believe I wasn't more confident when I was younger.

I'm caring and interested in others. I have time to listen to and be supportive. I am an empathetic person.

I haven't started to dye my hair yet. I'm a good friend. I'm proud of my kids and my home. I'm glad I try to do the right thing.

I always try to be self-aware. I like my consciousness. I am always trying to change things and I like risk-taking. I like to be provocative. I don't let myself down. I see myself as a really well-equipped survivor. Women constantly de-risk life, but I like taking risks.

That I don't feel jaded. I've had a lot of bad experiences and I have easily put them behind me.

When I teach I bring out the best in my students. And I can always find a bargain.

Everything about myself. I don't hate anything, or I would change it.

I can make people laugh when I need to.

I'm clever, but not too clever!

I like my spirit. That I am feisty. I'll fight for things. I have conviction and I am loyal. I like the causes that I get involved in. I like change. My creativity and my enthusiasm. I get very excited about stuff. I have fun. I like my strength and that I am flexible.

I like that I can help people. As long as I like you, I'll help you out indefinitely but, if you don't help me when I need it, you won't get my help again!

I like myself, I always have.

I feel a lot of love now and I am learning to show it.

I focus on the mundane and ordinary.

I am reasonably clever. I grasp ideas quite quickly. I am kind and thoughtful.

I am a very determined person, I don't give up. I'm a fighter to the end.

I am loyal and believe in good.

Extremely lucky.

That I have the ability to laugh at myself.

I'm not a perfectionist and I like that.

I am doing my best with my capabilities.

I get things done, I'm a doer.

The 50s

There's always a positive connection when I meet people.

I like to enjoy myself. I'm still badly behaved.

I am quick-witted. I like to make people laugh. I like that I can take the piss out of myself and can make people feel at ease.

I like everything about myself, body included.

I do like where I am right now, though it's had its moments getting here.

I like being international. I like being open to the world; all cultures, people and places. I am very relaxed where I am. My home is where my hat is.

I like a lot about myself. I like getting more confident as I get older and getting positive affirmations.

I am the archetypal Aphrodite.

I am a very spirited person who is quite adventurous and a risk taker. I really like that side of myself.

Feeling bright and discovering things you don't know.

That I am warm, supportive and determined. I like my efficiency, I like being interested.

I am a good listener. I am intuitive and have a get-up-and-go attitude.

I am happy and content in the fact that I am just an ordinary person.

I am an ageing women, vibrant with life and vitality.
Attractive, quite content and extremely lucky.

I have a pretty solid, strong sense of self: I'm not self-conscious, so I don't worry. I try to look forward not backwards. I am phlegmatic, I am a realist. I am good at living in the here and now. I'm not much of a planner. I am quite good at enjoying myself. I regard this as a reasonable talent.

I'm upbeat. I've always been like that. Life is too short. I haven't got any regrets. If I want to do something, I'll do it. There isn't anything I want to do. Except I'd like to go to Australia, but I don't like flying.

I really like myself. I'm seeing a more positive aspect of myself. I'm not expecting any negative impact and therefore always surprised when I get it:
'I didn't deserve that'.

People smile at me a lot, maybe because I smile at them.

I don't get depression, I have no time for depression. There's always someone worse off than me. I am happy with my lot.

I get on with people. I must be doing something right.

That I am a good mother, a good listener and creative.

I like that I am non judgmental and by just being calm and myself, it helps empower people. People open up to me, they feel confident and able to express their inner feelings to me. I love to challenge someone who is hardwork or aggressive, for some reason those types of people are drawn to me. I know once we've chatted, they feel calmer and more relaxed.

The 60s

I'm quite brave and confident. I always speak out. I provoke.

I don't lie, I'd rather offend than lie. I have a generous spirit. I am very nosey and I am interested in people. I get to the essence of people very quickly. I can tell a bullshitter when I see one.

I like the fact that people feel I'm approachable. What you see is what you get.

I'm a cheerful optimist; I get terribly excited by things. I like starting again.

I am completely happy in myself right or wrong. I love my own company.

That my intuitive, instinctive side is completely in the right direction.

I am compassionate, kind, loyal and I have a good sense of humour.

I love my own company; I love being with people, then I need to be on my own again.

I love going round bare-footed; if I could wander round the streets like that I would.

The 70s

Most everything really.

I like that I can make people comfortable in my home. I like that I attached more importance to people, not things.

I live in the moment. I'm glad that my friends have kept in touch since my husband died, it means I must be doing something right.

The 80s

That I have been able to absorb a good education.

I like that I am happy.

I love my family, all 11 of us. My family is most important,
that's why I nag them and want to see them.

That I am a reliable, tidy person.

The 90s

I am happy in my skin. You have to love yourself. I've always loved myself.
I have never felt dissatisfied about myself. Life wasn't always easy, but I took
it in my stride. I don't dwell, I just get on with it.

I like that I accept my age.

Remember not one negative please…

>> Our ever changing
Bodies

Why didn't my mum talk to me? I was so embarrassed. I bought my own sanitary towels. I never had enough underwear. I would hide the dirty ones in my drawer.

Childbirth was a real eye-opener, those classes make out there's just a bit of pain. I had pre-eclampsia and was hospitalised weeks before she came. I had to be induced and I started haemorrhaging. It was a scary.

I don't take HRT because I don't want breast cancer!

I had a coil fitted and bled for six months!

I've had years of hot sweats, I'm now on HRT. The physical heat is good, and emotionally I'm ok. My periods have stopped gradually. I've put weight on but then I eat a lot! HRT is good.

I lost a Tampax for six weeks, there was a very funny smell. I rooted around – the smell was awful. I went to the doctors. He found it. It was disgusting.

The first time I went on the pill, I put on a stone, felt revolting and had a period that lasted a month: best contraception out there!

What do you mean you want sex? I'm up to my eyes in breast pads and stitches!

I can only see the menopause as a wonderful transition into the next stage of life. It might not be pleasant, but it's all about change and growth.

The menopause ages you on all levels. 'Dried-out wrinkled old prune', that's how it makes me feel. I am embarrassed by the flushes, total humiliation that people can see you going through an old-age process. I feel much more invisible than I used to. It's so important to be visible.

The menopause is a huge part of ageing, it's a depressing part of being a woman, it's a sign of getting old.

Having a hysterectomy buggered my brain up.

August 24th 1986 Sharon in hospital, she's got anorexia

Stretch marks are a mark of motherhood.

We have a lot going on, stuff we put in and stuff that comes out. As women, we go through a lot, our bodies are constantly changing.

Being pregnant was very traumatic. I spent the first five months puking. I was hooked up to an IV drip.

Whilst I was playing netball at secondary school, my sanitary towel fell out onto the pitch!

I want to retreat into my cave and shed.

Days two and three of my period are unmanageable! No Tampax or pad can withstand the flow!

I feel my elasticity has gone in the last six months; dry skin, dry fanny, no sex drive. I'm slightly thinking, KY jelly!

When I had my miscarriage, I pulled down my knickers and there was my baby, 13 weeks old. I put it in the palm of my hand.

The most embarrassing incident. We were round at friends' for supper. As people arrived, I moved down to the next chair, slowly moving down to the end of the table. After doing this three times my friend kindly told me that I was leaking blood on her white leather chairs and her husband was surreptitiously cleaning up after me!

Looking at myself in the mirror and realising 'Shit, I'm in my 50s' and how others must see me. Physically, the hot flushes are insane, I am trying to stop resisting what is happening. I am truly accepting the fact that I am 51 and something's different.

I'm not looking forward to the menopause, it's a bit sad it's all ending. I can see that it could be liberating, a joy not to have periods.

It's hard what women have to put up with, there's such a lot to deal with and we still get on with it. We are quite tough, men would crumble. We are emotionally challenged.

I had a hysterectomy at 35 because of a fibroid that kept growing. I thought I'd turn into an old woman overnight. They were unfounded worries. I didn't have to have HRT. I had new vitality, it was a good thing. No periods or getting pregnant, it was all very positive.

October 25th 1999 Still hot sore nipples, feel cranky and tearful, eyes are awful!

What do you think about marriage?

Could we, should we, will we, won't we? Marriage often starts off as a lovely idea then over time can develop into hard work. It certainly doesn't make for the fairy tale scenario. It can be a test of tolerance, patience and compromise but, if you haven't done a runner, it seems it can grow into something altogether different which includes acceptance and admiration – if you're lucky. One thing is for sure, marriage isn't something that's going to fulfil or 'fix' us and it might be an idea to lower our expectations.

Here are their responses...

The 30s

It's lovely.

Two people coming together and trying to make a plan together.

It's communication: telling the world about it is an important rite of passage.

Getting married was everything I dreamed about, it was the most important day of my life. There's a feeling of security, togetherness, problems are 'together problems', you just can't walk out. A sense of unity. I quite like being 'Mrs X' with a ring on my finger. It's a big tick in your life box: marriage is wonderful!

The 40s

I must think it's a good thing, I'm about to do it for the third time! It's a source of emotional support.

We need grown-up support. The problem is, a lot of husbands become an extra child.

After 18 years I still can't decide if I think it's the right thing to do.

Oh, God! Too long! You need a change of scene. He's a wonderful husband. I am not an easy person to live with and when I want something done, I want it done now. He always tries to second-guess what I want. He cooks. Marriage I find stifling, tied down, restricting and caged!

It's a good thing if you marry the right one. I just didn't. I would do it again. It has to be a partnership.

I wish I hadn't married so young.

I never really aspired to be married, but I have a good partner and I've married him twice! The first time we were married for three years, then we got divorced and we were apart for 18 months. It was the most cleansing and cathartic thing I've ever done. We didn't have to be polite anymore. During the blow up we became more committed and stronger. We both thought we would do it again. The second time was private and quiet, it felt right, we were just more honest. Oddly, his parents married each other twice too!

I love my husband with a passion. I married my first love, we've been together since we were 17, almost 30 years. Although when I said 'I do', I didn't mean negotiate my arse off for the rest of my life. I like marriage, it's a good thing. I'm grateful I married my boy.

It's a useful institution. Two pairs of hands are better than one. It's nice to have a partner, I don't think it's the most natural state though. Men and women have different needs and wants. I don't think people are meant to be together for 50 years. He doesn't get from me what he needs and vice versa. Marriage is useful, it suits me.

Sometimes, I don't like the way he opens the curtains.

I like being married, I wish I'd got married earlier. He's allowed me to be the person I want to be. I don't know if the piece of paper means much. It's a commitment.

Marriage is difficult, I wouldn't do it again.

I hate obligation sex but if you don't sleep with your husband, someone else will.

I believe in marriage. A lot of people do it for the wrong reasons. It's a mad show of money, the idea of why you're getting married is lost.

I felt I have been the rock that's enabled him to do his thing.

It's the biggest risk you will ever take in your whole life. It's a learning game of give and take. Sometimes you have to do things you don't want to. It wasn't as easy as I thought it was going to be. You can't change someone, they are the person they are. As you get older, the respect kicks in.

It tore me apart when he had an affair.

I'm not that bothered by it, neither here nor there.
You're not guaranteed a happy relationship though.

I have been quite unhappy for a few years. I am resigned and learning to live with it. He is much older than me. He impinges on my space, he doesn't have boundaries. My need is to have space, I'm not afraid of being on my own. He's been a very positive influence in my life. We have a child which is a lasting connection and I'm bound to him.

We have both lost our get up and go.

I love it. It's all about trust and love.

Not to be entered into lightly by any stretch of the imagination. I don't regret it, it's a fantastic institution. It's the building block of society. I think it's best for children if their parents stay together. If there was an easy option I would have taken it by now. It's hard to extricate yourself once you've been with someone for so long. I didn't want to get married, it just made sense.

If you love your children, have the decency to love their mother/father too.

I'd done it once, I didn't really want to do it again. But I did! I don't think it's forever. I think people fall out of love. It should be more relaxed. It's so traumatic when people get divorced, it's best to keep the status quo.

I think it will get better.

It's the ultimate trust and hope for the future.
It's a contract: you don't know how long it will last.

I don't know what I think [sighing].

You can't have me unless you marry me. Women don't draw the lines clearly enough.

I want another go. I want to fall in love and start again. I might be having a midlife crisis. I want passion, I want to be in love. I have two choices, do I stay for the kids and get on with it, or chuck everything in? As soon as the children are gone, I'm out! He's taking the joy out of living.

My opinion has completely changed from when I was younger. It's a really important institution that safeguards your soul. The older I get, I realise that I need these ceremonies and institutions as anchors for the emotional thoughts I develop as I get older. It's a social construct for the family not just the two people involved.

It's not been top of my list although I always thought it was. I am frightened of it. I see it as an entrapment. One day I would like to be married, but I don't want to feel trapped by it.

I'm glad I'm married. I'm genuinely amazed that I still am.
I'm glad I can provide a stable family life.

I married him to get as far away from my parents as possible.

I really admire people who have the guts to leave. I wouldn't have the guts.

There's an Alan Alda film about marriage and how it's like going through the seasons. In the spring it's budding, in the summer there's heat and it's ripe, in the autumn it's maturing, and in the winter it dies. It has to go through death in order to have fun again.

He reads to me. I love listening to his voice.

My mum said to me, 'There are going to be times when you're married and you hate everything about him and you'll want to shoot him, but those days will pass. Don't think it's all going to be sweetness and light'. Romantic love as it is portrayed is utter triteness. Infatuation is great fun, but it isn't a marriage.

Having things in common has held us together. He opens doors.

We had a civil ceremony in 2006. We did it in order for me to get a visa. Marriage is good for long term couple-hood.

I think marriage is a good institution and you have to work at it. Don't take it for granted, remember why you got married. It does make you more stable.

I am married to a much older man. I want a partner that fulfils me in a physical way as well as through memories. I have a yearning to be with someone who has a shared childhood, memories like knowing who Starsky and Hutch are.

The 50s

It's all about trust and love. Marriage can be positively enhancing.
I never felt constrained.

When I said 'Shall we go fruit picking?' he said, 'Isn't that something you do when you're 16!'. With that attitude I'm not sure there's much hope.

It's a good thing. I should be married, I probably will be again. It's important in terms of confirmation or statement of faith.

I can't see how it could be better with a different person. Deep down, I am delighted with my children, they are a product of my marriage and that is my marriage. Marriage isn't necessarily the way I'd choose to live if there wasn't family involved.

I always assumed I would get married, my life improved once I got married. There had been so much sadness in my life and it only began to go once I got married. It was something clear to do after drifting for so long. I've had a brilliant marriage so far, I've remained myself, he's supported me continuously. We debate and argue, our marriage is very passionate, we get very heated. I think it's about having enough in common, communication and having the same values.

I am a simple person, I don't need a lot. My husband has moulded me and taken control over everything. I have allowed him to do it and I am bitter.

There's no such thing as a perfect relationship, you just have to doodle along.

The whole thing sounds tortuous!

It's a long haul, 27 years so far. It's good for the family framework.

August 3rd 1997 Bought wedding dresses in charity shop for kids to dress-up in

It's been great for me. It's hard work.

Life's all about family. I didn't want to get married but it's nice to have someone to moan to and to have fun with.

My husband said, 'Will you be my wife and mother of my children? But something has to give' - my career in the city.

Marriage is great. If you have been happily married it's probably harder to do it again because of high expectation of the next relationship.

There's no happy ending to marriage, it starts with happiness and ends in tears.

I didn't think I was going to get married. I was 29 when I did. He listens to me – you don't meet many men that listen to you.

It was quite fun whilst it lasted. I would do it again, surprisingly. Although there should be a handbook.

Name me someone who has a great life being married. Now name me someone who has a great life not being!

We are good friends. We don't argue much, but you know when one's coming.

We tell each other everything. I know him better than he knows himself.

Thirty-four years of being loved unconditionally – total love – to love and be loved is what I miss. [On being widowed]

Stay soft and nice and you'll end up with someone soft and nice.

It's hard work a lot of the time. I didn't have any doubts. I am very happy to be married. I would be terrified if my daughters didn't live with their partners first.

My mum died, I moved house and had a baby girl. Three stressful things. Then my husband decided to bugger off when she was ten weeks old. I believed in marriage for life.

I knew I never wanted to get married.

Marriage and co-dependant relations makes you try harder at your relationship. If you're single and you have a big blow out it's somehow easier to leave. As long as you can contain yourself within the marriage, it is so important not to lose a sense of who you are.

My mother always told me to marry someone who I would like to be my friend. I think she was absolutely right but I would add that it is also important to marry someone who had a good relationship with their mother. Personally I did not make the right choice, however I have two beautiful children and hence can have no regrets. In any event, I firmly believe that life offers you other opportunities for relationships and that the future is always open to more possibilities.

I was married for 29 years. He died suddenly from a heart attack. On reflection, marriage was a bit of a bore. There was an expectation that it was just what girls do.

Any good relationship equals compromise.

It would have to be an extraordinarily special man to make that commitment again. Marriage – it brings home to me that other people have to make compromises. I went from pleasing the parents to pleasing the husband. I became all roles – teacher, wife, parent. What about me, the one that needs other things to sustain me?

December 19th 2005 **There are advantages of marrying a chef, he cooked tea!**

He liked the girls and the fist!

I have been married for 43 years. Most of the time it's fine. There are times when I find him extremely irritating. I have evil thoughts, but we rub along nicely together.

Waking up the morning after I got married, I felt different, more secure.

You can change your mind.

The 70s

Never say anything against anyone's husband.

A vicar at the local church said, 'Marriage isn't about give and take, it's about give, give, give. But it only works when two people do it. For too many people, one person does all the taking.' We've been married 50 years. When I was younger, I was looking for more excitement. Now I don't seek it. I do like sameness and continuity. People are looking for too much. I was a virgin when I met my husband.

I don't think men and women should be tied together all their lives. You need a new spark every now and then.

We were married for 45 years. He worked hard, I can't say he didn't provide because he did, but he was selfish.

I didn't take to him at first, he was far too arrogant and full of himself.

It took me seven years to get over him leaving me. I threw myself into work then started to feel liberated. I started to have a good time. I think the family has broken down, fathers aren't around, there's not a unit anymore. Women have become too ambitious, leaving it late to have children. The family unit has changed its dimensions. Marriage is a wonderful thing if it works, but very few men seem to come up with what's needed. Men have been a bit of a let down.

I have been very lucky. I have known my husband since I was five. We have been together since we were 17. There's something in his eyes and face that I'll never get tired of seeing. He's the kindest, most generous man. He'd move heaven and earth for me.

I didn't think I would get divorced, we were married for 11 years.

I like the state of marriage. My partner won't marry me. There was a time when I thought he would. I only got divorced because I thought we would get married. We've been together for 40 years now.

The 80s

Marriage is very nice, sometimes it works and sometimes it doesn't. It's a lovely experience. I was sad we divorced and I'd never do him down. We were only married for 17 years, it wasn't long, he liked a flirt. I married again, he was a more stable man but sadly he died after only 9 years.

We are lucky we like the same things. We have friends who loathe each other. We read, he has a good sense of humour and he's a great friend. I always finish his sentences. I spoil him, he gets breakfast in bed every day. We have been married for 63 years. He did wander a bit, he had an eye for the pretty girls. It made me stronger, more determined.

Marriage is a good thing, it's 'proper'. I don't agree with two men or two women getting married. You have to work at marriage. People get fed up and think the grass is greener. A couple I know are about to celebrate 70 years of marriage.

I would have liked to have married and had children.
I didn't notice it so much then as I do now.

The 90s

I had 58 years of marriage. Not many men would have put up with me.
I always got my way. I was too independent.

We got married in St Thomas' Hospital a week before he died. He smoked 200
cigarettes a week so you can guess what he died from.

So what do you think about marriage?

Question 6

What do you think about children?

Children, love them or hate them? Have them or don't? The answers are full of contradictions. Children are a true polarity in life. A blessing, a wonderful creation and an amazing experience. But they are also exhausting, hard work, a huge responsibility, a major cause for worry but where would we be without them?

Here are their responses...

The 30s

I've always had a toddler in my life since I was six years old. Enough now!

Little babies are boring and I didn't seek enough help or company. We've lost a lot by not being part of an extended family. You lose something when you move away. Having children hasn't fulfilled me.

Having children is doing what I should be doing. The need to have children was intense. There are some things you just can't control. The desire to have children was overwhelming, nature just takes over.

If I had time again, I'd focus on being a mum and not on other things. I am staggered by the energy kids have and what they have taught me. They have exposed any falsity in me. My kids have made me become the real me. I always feel I've either done not enough or too much.

I thought I'd have two and I ended up with six. They are my life and soul, they are my breath. If I didn't have them I wouldn't be able to breathe.

The 40s

They are a vindication of a faith in myself. I am blessed with amazing children, they are proof that I am on the right track.

I love my children. They are little energy drainers, but you just get on with it. It's unquestionable, unconditional, part of the package. I have learned a lot and the main plus-point is that you have to put someone else before you which I can only say is a blessing. It makes you selfless and puts a different perspective on things. It's hard sometimes and it can be very boring, frustrating and exhausting, but I wouldn't be without them. No way.

**I was a subconscious box-ticker with a five-year plan until I had children –
that sorted that nonsense out.**

They aren't my world, but I have a lot of time and respect for them. I am amazingly
proud of my four. They should be screwed up after our break up but they're not.

Sometimes I need a lie down after an argument with the kids.

Children are amazing. Every single one of them a little miracle. I love kids.
They're hilarious. They think the world revolves around them. I'm glad I had
them. I still wish I was one.

Having kids was one of the reasons I got married.

Kids are a wonderful, a marvellous tonic. Pure unconditional love.
They are innocent. It's beautiful to watch life through their eyes.

**I am a great believer in children making their own decisions. They have to be
able to grow up, learn, and suffer the consequences. There's always a consequence
to everything you do.**

Life without children is unbearably self-centred, which is pretty rich coming from a
woman who vowed never to have children. I completely changed my mind. When I
was 18, I wanted to adopt. I had a 'there are too many children in the world' attitude.
At 21 I was terrified of getting pregnant but, at 27, a woman said to me, 'How can you
spend your whole life with someone without procreating, it's just not natural'. Until
that point I had never thought of myself as a natural being. Something happened at
that moment. It all started to make sense. Nature compels you to want to have
children. I don't like interfering with my body so I never went on the pill. I was having
sex, and my partner at the time didn't want children - that made me realise I did.

**There's nothing quite like a little hand in yours. Or a ten-year-old suggesting a
different outfit would look better, or, 'Mummy, you're too old to wear that!'**

Love 'em, hate 'em! It's like falling in love with somebody. It's so close you can't differentiate sometimes. Do we hate to love them or love to hate them? I am glad I had them. No-one ever told you it would be so difficult. My job is to make their lives the best they can be.

I wouldn't have chosen to have any. Being the eldest of seven, I'd done all the child-rearing I needed to. But I do have one, and I'd wish I'd had another for his sake.

The best thing I ever did in my life. I didn't mind if I didn't have a life partner but I wanted kids. It feels so much better to have a hug. Kids are a reason to exist, a responsibility. If you're lucky enough to have children, then there is always something positive in your life.

My life has gone on hold to do the children.

There's not a word strong enough to describe children. I love all the early bondings, the skin-on-skin, breast-feeding. That bloody Annabel Karmel cook book and those ice cubes. It was all a bit stressful!

All I wanted when I was a child was to be a mum.

Fucking annoying, hard work. Two's enough.

I've had two abortions. There are times when you do make a life-changing decision and having an abortion is one of them.

I never thought I wanted any, but I actually wanted more. It was so easy to get pregnant at 40 but then I miscarried three times. I felt peer pressure to have more.

My baby died when she was only a week old. I had never got on with my sister, but this time she said, 'I'm not going to tidy this one up'. It was a moment, one she didn't try to fix: she was just there for me.

Oh sweeties, I wish I'd had more, but not with my husband.
He's so negative and depressed. It doesn't make for a good example.

I really enjoy being a mum more than I thought I would and I'm better at it too,
although I'm a bit emotional and hysterical sometimes.

It's just love, joy and emotion.
More emotion than you can ever imagine or told you would have.

They are fantastic, although they drive me spare. Ignore all the shit that's out
there telling you what to do, how to bring them up and how you should be
feeling - trust your instincts.

I like them and the worlds they go into. They have vivid imaginations and no
inhibitions. The ability to express themselves in a very unconscious way. Their
innocence and naughtiness. They are the bedrock of our future. They are our
hope. They need lots of love and nurturing and the right food.
It was so not my path to have kids.

They are wonderful creatures, be prepared and surprised.
I'm delighted by them. The choices you make equals how you live.

Get yourself a doula [birth supporter], best money you can ever spend!

I love bringing my kids up but also love doing part time work. It's quite healthy
to have a balance.

I'm glad I had them, but I don't think they are for everyone. They are fucking
hard work - and expensive. They open you up to huge amounts of love and
pain. Love for your kids is unconditional.

The 50s

Having my daughter. She was two weeks late and I was induced and knackered before we'd even started. I was obsessed with not wanting to shit myself. I had the most fantastic epidural and an emergency C-section followed. For one reason or another, I ended up on a gurney on the hospital corridor with my baby tucked under my arms. Having a baby is a brutal shock to the system and no one prepares you.

I wanted four, but three's nearly killed me.

I always pop in to say goodnight even though they are asleep.

I'm happy I had kids. I wasn't maternal. I ran out of the pill and got pregnant.

I'd be missing something if I didn't have them.
I'm no earth mother but wouldn't be without them.

Kids are adults without the pretence and façade. They just 'be'. They haven't had conversations put on them yet. The older they get, the less interesting they become.

My son is 21 today. I am wondering if there is something I've forgotten to teach him. I became hysterical when he left home. I put myself to bed, my daughter said, 'Don't worry mum, it's just empty nest syndrome, it's going to last two years!'. 'No, it's not love.' I replied, got out of bed and headed into town and went shopping.

I wish I knew then what I know now,
then I would have enjoyed them when they were little.

Time again, I would have allowed toy guns in the house.

Support networks are vital.

I'm nostalgic for the kids when they were little.
They don't love me or need me like they used to do.

Amazing, exhausting, time wasters!

Glad I had them. I didn't think I wanted them. They are a very good grounder.
You see them changing and you have to adapt to that. It makes the passage of
time easier. If you don't have kids you are free to do whatever you want. People
get terribly set in their ways if they don't have kids, particularly if you are on
your own. Having kids is one whole accommodation!

I love and respect my children. I find the whole growing up thing a bit worrying.
It's a tricky business bringing up children, it's very easy to get it wrong.

Funny you should ask. This morning I spent 28 minutes asking my ADHD/
autistic child to put her shoes on. She'd go upstairs dilly dally about, then come
back down – still with no shoes on. I'd have had a cup of tea, made eggs on toast
and eaten them, and still she'd faff about!

I feel I was meant to have 5 children. I am probably a better older mum than I
was a younger mum. I like the fact we accept each other for who we are. They
know when I need my space and leave me alone. I've learned that what I might
want for my children isn't necessarily what they want for their lives, and actually
just because I'm their mum, doesn't mean that I'm right all the time.

My children are the most important people in my life. Having two children on
my own, life has been very busy but I have always tried and to a large extent
succeeded in having a life for myself with my own friends and interests.

There was a moment in the delivery room when I was thinking, do I really
want to do this, to look after someone else?

The 60s

I had this rather idealised image growing up of being like Jo in 'Little Women' and that I would run a children's home and it would all be wonderful. I do like being around children. I wouldn't have wanted to be without children in my life. I always wanted four but in the end only had three. I understand people who don't want children, I don't think it's selfish to make the choice not to have them.

I don't identify myself through my child.

An absolute pain and what a drain on you. You never get it right and I always make mistakes but I am very pleased I had them.

No-one should deprive themselves from being a mum. I've told my daughter I will help her if she wants to have artificial insemination if no man is around by the time she's ready.

The best thing I ever did. I did the usual, 'Aren't I clever, she's beautiful'. All the emotions. I couldn't stop looking at her.

Kids are a blessing, they reflect back on you. My son is teaching me even more compassion.

I was 20 when I had my first child. I would have liked to have experienced life a bit more first.

Kids are gorgeous - mothers are not!

I'd love to bring my son and daughter together; they don't talk and haven't for ten years.

The 70s

I know the joy we truly get out of our younger generation.
I enjoy the presence of youth. Old people are so miserable.

I love my children and having a grandchild is the icing on the cake.

My children are my prime motivation in life.

I get a lot of pleasure from my children and my grandchildren.

Being a mum is the best thing anyone could be.

The 80s

I was always aware of health issues that surrounded my family. My aunt died
from diabetes; there was a lot of asthma and rheumatism in our family. My dad
had to have his leg amputated because of his diabetes and I couldn't see what
the future held so I decided I didn't want to bring children into the world.

We were very much expected to have had our first child by the time we were 28,
that's just how it was. I'm glad I had my two girls although I would have liked a
boy too.

Being a grandmother is the peak!

I love my role as grandmother. I think they see us as an elderly couple who have
a swimming pool and send them nice presents at Christmas and birthdays.

I loved having them when they were babies.
What would the world be without babies?

October 1st 1998 **We have a new baby girl, Anna.**

The 90s

I have loved having my four children.

I had a stillborn baby boy, there were no tears shed!

What do you think about children?

Question 7

Where does all your energy go?

Energy taking it in or giving it out - where does it all go? I'm not sure anyone thinks what their energy goes on but we do use a lot of it. Based on these responses, it seems we waste quite a bit. If we aren't preserving our energy, is it any wonder we become depleted?

Maybe if we looked after our own energy supplies then the planet might be in a better state.

Here are their responses...

April 29th 1997 My back's hurting a lot - result of pressure hosing the patio!

Husband

Worrying Myself Walking Living Expelling Rushing Giving

Relationships Housework Feelings Thinking Being intellectual Spending Running Driving

Dissatisfaction Singing Daydreaming Projects Chilling Wasting time Exercising Facebook

Being tired Being resentful Children Sitting in traffic Exhausting myself

My self destruct button Not going with the flow Being healthy Connecting with people

Being old makes it difficult sometimes Feeling pressured My mind Sitting My thoughts

Sex Caring Creating Struggling Frustrations Sabotaging myself Taking on too much

Voices in my head Organising My job Pleasing others Listening Work Cooking

Anger Being healthy Flapping Friendships Menopause Talking Feeding Masturbating

Emotionally being drained Being a control freak Gardening eBay Taxiing Socialising

Family I give too much away It all takes energy! …

What do you do with yours? _____

>> Who likes Shoes?

I got me some Louboutin shoes – £400!

The most important thing is comfortable shoes.

I'm a shopaholic for trainers and shoes, I have two shoe racks full. I'm terrible. I buy them and don't wear them – they are still in the boxes.

It used to be an obsession: I used to hate my body and shoes never let you down. Your feet never change size. Shoes are pretty things removed from all the psychology of clothes.

I can't believe I am still hiding stuff from my husband!

Shoes are an art form. I have between 120 and 130 pairs. Then there are my top-end shoes which get special treatment.

The first thing I did when I fancied a man was to look at his shoes. If they didn't come up to scratch, then there was no way! I would pursue the man by the size of his foot: adequately large. I don't like men with small dainty feet, their feet need to be manly.

People present their personalities through their shoes; shoes express the way you greet the world.

I have too many shoes. It's the one constant thing. All my life my weight has fluctuated, my shoe size hasn't. I love them with a passion. Last year, I was clearing out my wardrobe and found my £600 Gina pony skin stilettos - the moths had eaten them. It was a mini bereavement. It was my fault and I had to throw them out. I miss them deeply.

I love shoes but I have lymphoedema, and therefore they are a problem purchase

I could buy shoes every day. I have over 100 pairs. When I take them out of the box, I stroke them. I show them off to my family.

The shoes I have, I love. I can't get boots to fit me. The zip's gone in a pair of boots but I love them so much. I'm going to have to throw them away.

I'm not into shoes, but I love boots. I have a fantastic pair of boots up to my knees in cow hide. My purple boots are my faves. Would you like to see them? Boots have different personalities.

Arthritis has ruined my shoe choice.

I'm a size nine, I can't get shoes to fit!

I have so many pairs of shoes, it's embarrassing. I am beginning to realise I have more than enough and I don't need any more.

Shoes have to be comfortable, which tells me I am middle-aged.

Two things you should spend your money on, a good bed and a good pair of shoes, 'cos if you're not in one you're in the other.

I'm ashamed how many pairs I have. I've so many crippling shoes, it's sinful.

I don't mind suffering for nice shoes.

I always buy two pairs of the same shoes, one in blue, one in black. I am matching obsessed, matching handbags too.

I love pretty shoes. Back home in Trinidad, I was famous for wearing the latest shoes. The man in the shoe shop would put aside the latest ones in a box marked with my name on, just for me.

I buy loads of shoes. I buy them but don't wear them. I have over 40 pairs. Comfort is key.

March 19th 1998 Tommy Balls for shoes - cheapo Clarks shoes £1.50 a pair — bargain!

Question 8

What are your dreams?

Most of these answers were simplistic and very achievable, if not already achieved. That for me, along with the weather question that's comimg up, is the beauty in what I've taken from my project. Uncomplicated answers that don't make for sensational reading are the perfect antidote to the world we're living in. These women have small-scale ambitions and dreams. They come from a kind, nurturing and creative place. The media plays on our fears and insecurities and would have us believe we live in a terrible world with terrible people. Wouldn't it be lovely if we could hear daily reminders from everyday women about how for the most part, they just want to be in the here and now with what life is putting in front of them? To be around nature and to nurture and to have simple and achievable goals? Bliss!

Here are their responses...

The 30s

To become a mum.

To be out of London, living in the country with animals and a family.

Being still, finding a still place inside that gives you the freedom
to be brave and take risks.

I would like to be more OK with the ordinary. As a child, I wanted to be a travel
journalist; I loved writing stories. I need connection for my own sense of well-being.

I feel I'm on the right track. I wanted a good husband and children, to live and
work in London, and everything I wanted has happened. Just to keep it all
going is good enough.

My goal is to find inner stillness, so I can override the waves better.

I'd like to be financially secure, pass my driving test and get a car.

The 40s

I'd love to live in Cornwall – I crave the countryside -
and to live in a therapeutic community.

I'd like a house in the country. It's not a frustration, it's an aspiration. I'd like to
live in a middle-class village with a summer fête, join the W.I. [Women's
Institute]. The garden is wonderful, there are dogs and a Land Rover. There's an
area for the muddy boots in the hallway and an Aga where I can take time to
bake and to do something industrious.

My dream is to help reconnect people with their own health and heart.

I would like a smallholding on an organic farm in the middle of Scotland,
living in scruffy clothes and wellies.

I'm looking to be fulfilled outside the family unit. I need to find something
challenging in work. I am thinking about the children leaving, and life as a
couple. I'd like to create something that was well-loved. I've always wanted to
sing in a band; I'm a bit of a rock chick at heart.

Intimacy with someone you really like, no agendas.

Keeping the boat afloat; it's the everyday that makes me tick.

My friend gave me a plaque with the words 'All I want is world peace and thin
thighs' - it's flippant and idealistic but it sort of sums me up. I'm less concerned
about thin thighs these days.

I am emotionally ambitious; you have a responsibility to better yourself
emotionally. I write things down and when I re-read back it's that what makes
me happy but I'll keep hoping for world peace.

I did always fancy being a ballet dancer.

I like the idea of helping someone through their death and utilizing my compassion.

I'm really satisfied with my life; I don't have a dream that needs filling at the moment.

Sitting in the garden, feeling absolute contentment,
especially when I've had a fulfilling day.

Having my family is and was my ultimate ambition. It's my life's great work, I don't really care about anything else. I needed to be a mother and the best mother I can possibly be.

My dream is to have time. Oh, and £1000 to go shopping, and a personal trainer.

I'm a suppressed thrill-seeker, I just wish I had the confidence to do it.

I would love to live by the sea, to sit on the beach and watch the sea. Escape, fresh air and freedom.

I always wanted to work in a cheese shop.

Espresso, red wine, open conversation and adventure.

I'd like my life to be more predictable and settled so I can make choices I want to make, rather than ones I have to.

To live in France and potter about. A rustic, rural place, an idyllic shutter house. If I feel down or in a bad place I always go to France in my head. It's a perfect house, calming, and I'm on my own.

I dream of owning a cake shop.

Now, I would have liked to have considered university, but I never even explored it as an option.

For my daughter not to be incontinent; to find an equilibrium and know the right thing to do.

My dream path is running parallel to the one I am on.

I dream of clear floors. There's stuff everywhere, I don't sort things out. I'm embarrassed and used to make excuses about my house. I cringe and my stomach feels funny about the idea of somebody seeing the mess. I feel I've let my children down. The untidiness has a function, it's my security blanket.

The 50s

I have fantastical adventurous dreams about horses and handsome men!

I don't have any dreams, I am happy with my lot. I am fulfilled and content – family and health is everything.

To meet a man and connect on all levels.

My passion is flowers. If I had the money, I'd have a little coffee shop that sells flowers.

Being amazed by the beauty around me. Making myself a bowl of porridge and a cup of green tea, savouring the moment!

I dream of a little house in Norfolk, going back to childhood, my own space, something of my own.

I feel blessed already!

Sometimes kids are a lost voice. I would love to be a foster parent.

To live by the sea; it's so calming and relaxing.

Being around a camp fire – there's something about a fire that keeps me there.

I dream of being less busy, but content.

To be able to laugh at myself.

My passion is meditation. I start every day by saying 'Hello'.

I'd like to be married to a craftsman. A fantasy partner, a man with skills. I am absolving responsibility really, I want someone else to do it for me.

Why do you have to have a dream? Why not look around you? It's not perfect but so what?

I am quite fortunate in that I don't need much. I'd like a nice home near water. Where you live is all about the people I rely a lot on the people around me.

When I get off the plane back home in St Lucia, I can see the hills – my mountains – I am encased, they can't send me back, I'm home.

I would love to live in an eco house with bees.

The 60s

I want to make lots of noise. Play loud music all the time. I want goats, pigs, loads of chickens and a treehouse just for me.

I'd really have liked to have been a window-dresser or a sign-writer.

My fantasy is that I am so strong that, if anyone is aggressive, I can do karate moves and leave them flat on the floor.

To continue this next phase of my life, the best stage of my life. I have a project in Trinidad, I have seven acres of land where we have a house. The dream is to have an open house for friends and artists, a sanctuary, a retreat.

The 70s

My passion is dancing. Dancing frees your mind, but it's the music that sets your body free. I went to the Royal Academy of Dance until I was ten. I had a huge opportunity, but we just couldn't afford it.

The 80s

I'd love to have lived on the left bank of the Seine in France during the Sixties. I read a lot about the artists, the freedom to do what you want, it was a Bohemian lifestyle. I like that idea.

Homeless people always worry me. I'd like to build some kind of shelter and enable the homeless to help themselves.

To continue to do the simple things, to physically get up, get dressed and get myself to Sainsbury's.

The 90s

There's not much I want or need but sometimes the thought of a certain food, one I haven't had for a while can make me dream for that taste.

What are your dreams? What makes you tick?

Question 9

What's your most memorable experience?

We all have millions of memories but, in order to come up with the most memorable one today, it's got to be the one right there in your head. The one you've already thought about as soon as you read the question. It might be obvious – and many were – the registry of life: births, deaths and marriages. But some seemingly came from nowhere and caused pause for thought. Confusion as to why 'that' memory was still in there.

Asking this question gave time for reflection. The feelings that these memories provoked. The embarrassment and guilt, the joy and grief, pain and confusion, along with the sensual memories that go way back and are lodged somewhere deep down.

The wealth of experiences these few women have is overwhelming so you can only imagine what the whole world's experience has to offer. Memories, when shared, invoke humility, compassion and sincerity. By hearing we are feeling the essence of these experiences.

Here are their responses...

The 30s

Losing my grandad. He was the glue, an amazing man. We would go off and sit for hours and hours and chat. He was Jamaican, he had a lot of time for people, he had real words of wisdom. I miss him.

I was beaten up by my ex. I knew I didn't want to be with him. I was trapped in my own house. He psychologically bullied and threatened me. I was scared for our son. Once, he kicked me in the head, there was so much blood. It was horrid. Really horrid.

Giving birth to all my three children. This is what life's about! I would happily do it again and again. Everything I do is trying to relive that wonderful experience. It's a feeling of purposefulness, creation in the moment. Having a baby is literally an out-of-body experience. I am doing what I should be doing. There are some things you just can't control and the desire to have children was overwhelming, nature just takes over.

Giving birth is a powerful memory. After she was born I felt I could do anything, 'I am invincible'.

I had a nervous breakdown earlier on this year. I was so scared. I don't cry, but I cried a lot, I felt so fucking terrible. It was panic crying; it didn't help, but it was a release.

I was pregnant at 16 and I didn't tell anyone. I was scared to tell my Mum. More scared than actually giving birth. I was at home, in the toilet knowing something was happening. The baby's head was coming out and I was trying to push it back up whilst my Mum was banging on the door and shouting,
'What's going on in there?'

The 40s

Being thrown out of my flat onto the street in my underwear by my ex. He was a lazy, violent, alcoholic. I had to go into a women's hostel; it saved my life.

When I was pregnant I was unbelievably excited, it was every Christmas all rolled into one! Then a labour of 72 hours. I definitely thought I was going to die. An emergency C-section followed – it wasn't the chapter I was expecting. Later, I was stood in the corridor of the hospital where tears and milk were just pouring out of me.

Being woken at three in the morning to find my dad was being taken to hospital; he'd had a massive heart attack. He died shortly after.

Just after my daughter was born. Wondering what you do with a new baby. This little tiny face, her tiny eyes. It was an instant bond, a feeling stronger than love. A sweet moment.

Telling my sister at the airport that our dad had committed suicide.

I was 19, my parents decided to move abroad. I could have gone with them, but I chose not to. I had a heavy feeling in my heart and no understanding of the impact this would have on me, or the repercussions. In one way I felt so liberated from them and, in another, so sad they'd gone. I felt very uncertain.

I have a very vivid memory of my mum and dad arguing. I was three. We were just about to eat, the table was set with delicate cut crystal glasses filled with strawberries and cream; she threw one at him.

A walk I took a few years ago, along hedgerows near the south coast. It was a beautiful autumnal day, the sky was blue and the sun was out. Huge, red berries on the trees. Beautiful. I remember just looking and feeling very romantic. If I'd have been a poet I'm sure this would have been a perfect opportunity to write something poetic.

I have many memories of my walks from Santiago de Compostela. I go most summers. It's the experiences you have along the way and the people you meet. I met a woman with a shaved head, a natural lady, knapsack on a stick over her shoulder, a bit Dick Whittington. She was a proper pilgrim, she slept under trees, beneath the stars, doing the walk in a very basic way. She had no fear.

The birth of my first son. It's the best moment of my whole life. I always wanted to be a mum, I always thought, 'I'll grow up and have lots of children'. My life has now changed for ever.

I remember sitting under an apple tree, I was about seven. I had rolls and rolls of wallpaper and off-cuts of carpet. I made a home under the tree, then I dressed the tree. It was during the summer holidays. I worked all day on this project and I remember completing it, stepping back and thinking, 'Look what I have just done'. It was a beautiful day and I was so happy and content.

Getting married. I was 30. The spinster of the village. There was a huge family expectation that I should have been married, but I wanted my career first.

We moved house when my mum and dad split up. We had to get rid of the family dog. Then we inherited two cats in our next house. My sister became allergic so they had to go too. When it was time for them to go, I kept pulling their fur out to try to hold on to them. It was very traumatising; I felt lonely and lost. You confide in animals, you tell them what's on your mind, you love them.

Before we had kids my husband and I went to New England. We were sitting under a wooden canopy on a jetty listening to 'Driftwood' by Travis. It's the most relaxed I've ever been. It was autumn, my favourite time of year. Everything was just right, fresh air on my face, no timescale. Bliss!

My Mum hugging me properly for the first time and me allowing her to do it. She was 77. It's only when you are a parent yourself that you realise how special that bond is and therefore realise when you haven't had it!

Being in hospital when I was 14. I had something called Poland Syndrome, which for me meant having my one of my breasts reconstructed. The drains were tied to my chair and I would forget they were there. Every time I got up; the pain…it was horrific, it hurt so much. You'd think once I'd done it once I wouldn't do it again, but I kept on doing it over and over.

When the doctor said 'mastectomy'. He dragged the telling me process out. I'll never find a man now. I'll be mutilated. I'd always been confident about my body and my sexuality. A feeling of sheer horror, not to do with the cancer, but my body image.

I was 28 and a reporter for Sky. I'd never done live TV before and due to someone not turning up last minute, I was pushed to the front line and had to do a live broadcast. I was furious, shocked and scared but the sense of pride and achievement when I did it was fantastic.

Sitting on the top of the roof of my Renault 5 with Beethoven blaring out. I was 20. It was spring and I was surrounded by fields of rapeseed. I was on my own for once. I had gone there in a fury. Lying there watching the clouds; that feeling that you're aware that you're really happy.

The month that followed having my daughter, there was a clan of women in the house: aunts, sisters, girlfriends. Cooking, cleaning, feeding, a whole team. It was a real woman's camp and I felt so cared for. This time was magic, every moment felt like a day.

I was working as a florist in Manchester and there was a job advertised in the Manchester Evening News for a florist in Bermuda, I applied and got it! I was 33 years old and it was 1997. I lived in Bermuda for seven years, where I subsequently met my husband. We got married there in 2003.

I got run over when my daughter was two. It was a very humbling experience being in a wheelchair and not knowing how long I would be in it for. Not being able to cook or do anything. I realised just what an impediment being disabled can be.

The 50s

I passed my driving test; it was my first truly elated feeling of achievement.

Driving in a car, first year at university with a guy friend that I really fancied. I felt happy – it's a rare feeling to really notice it. Being completely in the moment, it's a very sensuous feeling.

My mum died in 1992 from cancer. I was 29. It was six months from diagnosis to death.

We went on holiday last year to Thailand to stay with a very old school friend. He died suddenly six months later. It was very surreal, we'd just been there. I had known him 35 years.

We lived in Africa. I was eight. My parents and I were waving my sisters off to go back to boarding school in England after the Easter holidays. There was something on the runway, an obstruction. Instead of taking off the plane lost control. At the end of the runway was a 30 ft drop, the plane went over the edge. The whole thing went up in flames. There was a terrific smell of burning flesh and aviation fluid. We watched the whole thing. My two sisters died, along with many others. I remember my dad running down the runway as fast as he could, but nothing could be done.

I remember one time sitting barefoot under a mango tree back in St Lucia, smoking a spliff. I was reading the Qur'an. It was a beautiful day and a relaxed moment.

Giving birth to my daughter. Twenty-two years later it's still crystal clear. An extraordinary range of emotions, pain and anger. I don't think I've ever felt anything so intense. It was 24 hours that I don't think I could repeat.

I was living in Africa and was sent to boarding school in England to do A-levels. I had no choice. It was really awful. I comfort ate then became anorexic.

Getting married. So much good and so much bad. I had a lot of ambivalence whether it was the right thing to do. I did what I said I would never do: 'Marry me, or I'm leaving you'.

When I was 17 I had an abortion by C- section; I was 18 weeks pregnant. I put myself in a bubble and detached. I just got on with it.

When I was 19 my brother and I took a trip to Nepal. It took us two-and-a-half months by public transport and all we had was 200 quid. It was a fascinating year off. It was the time of the hippy trail. We went by bus and train from London to Venice, on to Istanbul, then another bus to Afghanistan, a train along the Khyber Pass and onto Delhi. We really bonded.

I remember when my grandad was ill, he would gather honeysuckle and fennel and bathe in the petals.

Meeting my husband, knowing at that moment we were going to be great mates. It wasn't love at first sight but there was an instant connection.

Once I was sat in the car just looking and watching people. There was a sense of real peace inside me. It was as though I was observing everything from a different perspective. It wasn't from my physical being, if that makes sense. It was a moment when I felt as though I was on a different vibration.

Going on holiday to Ireland with my soon to be father-in-law, his cousin, and a friend. For some reason my boyfriend couldn't come. We took a road trip, driving around Ireland for four weeks in my VW Beetle. By the time I got home, I felt like I was personally responsible for the potato famine. We had lots of fun and I certainly got to know my father-in-law. He couldn't cope with me, he thought I was 'too open and too honest'.

The 60s

When I was very small, I remember walking into our local village with my teddy bear. My Mum said, 'If you get tired of carrying that teddy, I'm not carrying it'. He ended up in the ditch on the roadside.

My first baby was stillborn at eight months.

I was brought up in East Africa. We lived on a hill looking over Lake Victoria. It was the colonial era. It left the biggest impact, and most things I do now from my home in London are based around Uganda.

First time I made love to my husband (he was my boyfriend at the time) in a scrappy little flat in Berlin. Such gentleness. We spent a whole year in bed. I felt so guilty because we should have been doing stuff and achieving but, when I look back, it was the best year of my life.

My husband's death. I was 27, I had two small kids. He drowned on a building site. I've learned to live with it but I'll never forget. If it's a Tuesday morning and it's raining, I look at the clock. I took too many tablets and ended up in the mad house for a few days.

I worked at the Foreign Office. This particular morning, I opened a letter containing an incendiary device!

On holiday a few years ago. I was standing at Pearl Harbour in Hawaii – I cried, and I have no idea why.

I was in the National Gallery in London looking at the pictures. It was just a feeling I had. I was alone and it felt really special to be there all by myself in that space. Afterwards I walked out into Trafalgar Square with that feeling, 'All's well with the world'.

Losing my sister this year. It's still too recent and very raw.

Having my daughter. I had a male student midwife, which was quite something in the Sixties.

My best friend died when she was 16. I had a visit from her in a dream. You're very lucky if you have a visit.

When I was eight, dad was posted to Singapore. We sailed on a troop ship for three weeks from Southampton. I distinctively remember the smell on the liner of oil and heat, it was very exciting. We spent three years there.

When I was four, I went to a tiny convent boarding school. I loved the nuns. During my time there I learnt about book-binding, using an old fashioned method of flour, cloves and water. We used to bind the hymn books. Book-binding became part of my life. I have the convent to thank for making me independent.

We went to live in Nigeria in the Sixties with my husband's job. The head of state had been shot and there was a public execution of the people who had done it. We didn't go, but the morning after it happened we were walking along the beach and saw the three stakes where the bodies had been, their shoes just lay there. It was shocking.

Seeing my dad on an oxygen cylinder. He didn't have a penny to his name. He'd been posted to Belsen after the war to do the clearing up. He had really bad chest problems and contracted emphysema. He died at 58.

The 70s

My happiest times are here, in my home, thinking how lucky I have been and am. There's real peace here. I am happy with my dogs, watching the birds. Simplicity and peace. No nattering. I am at one with nature and myself.

I had two sons from my first marriage, then adopted two Sri Lankan girls with my second husband. I can't believe how happy I was, my life was perfect, then he changed. He left me for someone else and it was really hard. It took me seven years to get over it.

In the war, my parents lived abroad and I was brought up by my grandma. It was the day they were coming home. I had been naughty and my gran had put me in the corner. I didn't want them to see me in trouble so I started to eat the glass tea set from my dolls' house and cut my mouth open. I'd do anything for attention. I created a drama, which is what I wanted.

I gave my son away. I was pregnant at 17 and unmarried, it wasn't what you did. I had no choice. Imagine giving your baby away, it was sheer horror and very traumatic. Twenty-five years later he got in touch, having him back was nearly as traumatic as giving him away.

I was born in Hendon during the war, both my parents both worked in the ammunition factory based locally. A bomb went off in our street and the glass in our conservatory shattered everywhere. My dad told me I'd been in my crib just a few minutes before and for some reason he decided to take me out of the room. Although it's not my memory, it's a story I remember from being a child and if my dad hadn't moved me I wouldn't be here talking to you.

I was 21 and it was the summer of 1962. My dad was working in the film industry, – he was a sound engineer and had worked on a lot of big films: 'Fiddler On The Roof', 'Bridge on the River Kwai'. This year he was in Rome filming 'The Taming Of The Shrew' with Elizabeth Taylor and Richard Burton. I spent the summer with him. I met Elizabeth Taylor, she was very small, she was friends with my dad. One evening she came over to talk to him, she looked me up and down, she wasn't that friendly. It's only looking back on it that I realise it was quite a special time.

My son getting divorced was worse than my husband getting cancer.

I was sent to boarding school, I was four-and-a-half! You can't judge it because you don't know any different. I instinctively knew something wasn't right but I couldn't express it any other way than just being desperately unhappy. I could never understand my parents. I don't know why they would do such a thing. I never blamed them for sending me away though I never felt a bond with my mother – when I look back I think she suffered with depression. Experiences in life make you who you are.

The 80s

During the Blitz, my gran lived at Waterloo. There was a raid on, everyone went into the shelter, my gran didn't want to go; her neighbours had been mean to her, they said she'd taken up two seats last time she'd been in the shelter and it was because she was so fat. It was her saving grace. The shelter was bombed and everyone died, all her street, her neighbours, her community. It's right where the Young Vic [theatre] is now; I think there's a plaque.

Splitting up with the father of my children. I think of it as a failure. Perhaps I didn't pay him too much attention.

During the war we took the tram to Purley Downs. Whilst walking, we could hear a low-flying plane. We could even see the bloke in the cockpit, he made a gesture with his hand, he opened fire – we were thrown to the ground. My dad dived on top of me as machine gun pellets were hitting the ground all around us. They missed, but could have easily hit us. It was just like a scene from one of those war movies. There had been a Daily Mail article about machine-gunning children which hadn't done much for morale, so these incidents weren't talked about, but they happened.

When your husbands die! Both mine have died from heart attacks at home. I've had to do the kiss of life and chest-pumping twice.

I was evacuated to Chichester when I was ten. I shared a bed with the family's daughter. Her father was a lorry driver. They only bathed once a week. I was quite shocked as I had come from a middle-class family and we bathed regularly. I had been out for a walk. When I came back I was told that my mum and younger sister, who was five, had died. Our house back in London had been bombed. Our dog survived. I would cry myself to sleep.

The 90s

When I was ten, I had typhoid fever. I went into a coma. I had a vision there were stairs going up and up and up, getting narrower near the top. A blackbird dropped a silver chain on my chest and, at that moment, I woke.

In 1955, I took my daughter on one of the last banana boats from Trinidad to Liverpool. It was a three-week crossing over the Atlantic.

There are so many memories but I do remember the first time I saw my daughter, she was born upstairs in my house in 1942. It was a time when you had to stay in bed for two whole weeks after giving birth. It was so boring.

What's your most memorable experience ?

Question 10

Who or what inspires you?

What are you inspired by? For a few of these women there were the obvious famous people, like the Oprah Winfreys of the world – actors, singers and inspirational people who had stood for something or achieved a quest of some kind, but for most, it was the everyday inspirations. We are often taught that inspiration comes from innovation, success, achievement and an unachievable ideal that the 'normal woman' cannot reach. Thankfully, we can see through all that. The responses were inspirational in their ordinary, accessible and achievable way.

Here are their responses...

My Mum Open spaces Get up and go Gardens Mountains Hills Smells Trees Flowers Kindness Art People Women Fantasy The human mind Oprah Winfrey Taste Goodness The sea History Water Cats Taking risks People who make a difference Fabric Sunsets Old Buildings Honesty Stars Frank Sinatra The marathon Animals Waterfalls Real people My teacher Creativity My dad The rain Landscapes Womens refuge Non conformists The Dice Man People that constantly challenge themselves My family Nature Alice Walker Shirley Williams People that work with disabled kids Elements Words of wisdom 'Hope' by Watts People who over come adversity Judy Dench Intelligence Adagio in D minor Self motivation...

…My parents Colour Good orators

The outdoors My gran The bleakness of Scotland Mastering a skill The Vatican My friend

Writers Explorers Collecting shells on the beach Unfurling ferns Weather The Beach

The Spring A leaf Craggy coves of Cornwall Speaking another language Life

My sister The seasons Queen Elizabeth 1st Nesting wrens Journalists Olympians

Thich Nhat People who give up their freedom to contemplate Friends Truth Transformation

Fashion The smell of lavender Harriet Lamb My in-laws The River Thames The WI Moss

Artists The smell of coffee Ken Robinson Exhibitions Geniuses of the world Tea Dreams

Quizzes Wild flowers Food My grandchildren Jasmine oil Creative minds Old Plane song

Hair Ordinary people The smell of a good book Humanity Sand

Confidence Edward Lear Poetry Sand Mo Mowlan North Korea Mouse paws Thunder

Lighting a candle Winston Churchill My mother in law Break Break Break by Tennyson

Peter Tatchell Adventurers People who speak out Boat builders Choral music Change

Scenery The smell of ground pepper Matt Pritchett Buddhist monks Young people

Enthusiasm Energy Tommaso Maccacaro My students Beautiful places Maggie Smith

Musicians Leaves Sunlight Mary Seacole Marie Curie Mrs Thatcher Gershwin Tenderness

Rain forests Animals and their quirky behaviour…

What are your inspirations?... _____

>> Fancy a bit of...
Chocolate?

I love it so much I don't buy it.

Chocolate is my aphrodisiac – it makes me relax. It gives me spots, but I'd rather deal with the spots than what I have to think about.

I've given it up for January. I love it, I miss it, but I'm going to be having some in February.

An absolute must. Chocolate makes me smile, it makes me laugh. I love chocolate. If I eat a Double Decker; I bite off the biscuit bit at the bottom, then I'm left with the nougat. I roll it into a ball and put it in my mouth, so my mouth is so-o-o full!

It's the 'snap' sound I love.

It tastes better when your mouth is full. When I eat a Toblerone, I put the whole triangle in, it's uncomfortable and it hurts my gums and cheeks, but I like it.

Really dark chocolate every day. Three or four squares when I need energy or a treat! I feel it's an invasion if my husband has stolen it!

Food is an effort, chocolate is a pleasure.

My Mum used to make chocolate sandwiches; a bar of chocolate and white bread.

I was addicted to chocolate, I couldn't go without it. I would eat a jar of Nutella every day when I first came to live in London – it must have been a comfort thing. I had to go cold turkey.

December 19th 1984 Made chocolate digestive fridge cake

I have this thing that I do. When it's Easter, I peel the silver foil from a Cadbury's egg – the biggest I can find and put it over my face. Then I sniff it, really hard. You can only do it once, then the smell has gone. It's a real chocolate hit. I've always done it. I try and get my kids to do it but, for some reason, they don't feel the same!

I love it! It's rich, sensual, satiating, a wicked pleasure that melts into you.

I have chocolate everyday. I can't live without it.

I make a chocolate salami – chocolamis! Which is dark chocolate, cherry, pistachio, cranberry, shortbread biscuit and Amaretti biscuits. Delicious.

It's fantastic, magical, an absolute necessity. It's the best drug on the market. I love it more than alcohol. I use it to close the day's activities. When I eat chocolate, it opens up my mind to dreams, I glide somewhere else at that moment.

OMG, I can't live without it. It would be my desert island luxury. It's always in my fridge.

I love it, high quality, small amount of nice chocolate. I'm a chocolate snob, I don't do Cadbury's. If I am given a box of chocolates, I find it difficult not to eat the whole lot.

It gives me indigestion, but I still eat it.

Chocolate is very exciting!

All my life I have loved Fry's Chocolate Cream, ever since my childhood. I'd always have a bar of Fry's in my handbag, and I loved the end piece even more because the chocolate was thicker. I used to like Black Magic too. In the tuck shop at school I would rush to get the gobstoppers and pineapple chunks and sit at the back of the class with my cheeks full of toffee.

October 8th 2005 Made chocolate fondue and fruit kebabs with the kids.

Question 11

How do you feel about the weather?

When I asked 'How do you feel about the weather?' most women gave me a look as if to say, What? You're really going to ask me about the 'weather?' Most definitely; it had to be here. It's the one topic we all talk about. It's the ice-breaker. My Mum mentions the weather throughout most pages of her diaries. Everyone talks about it. It's something certain and uncomplicated. The answers reflected that and having asked a seemingly dull question, I was fascinated and intrigued by some strong, even poetic views.

Here are their responses...

The 30s

I love rain, but what I really love is lying in bed listening to it.

The weather is a biggie. If I lived anywhere else it wouldn't be.
It's such appalling weather where we live.

I do like the sunshine. I like the seasons, I like weather to change.
I love the feeling of heat, it defrosts you.

Smells matter to me. Smelling the air affects my sense of well being. The way the
seasons smell settles me.

The 40s

It changes moods. We talk about it far too much because it changes so much.
It affects what you do. I like being inside when it's pouring outside.

London would be the best place in the world if it was picked up and put some
place south of Bordeaux.

I dislike autumn, it's dishonest because it signifies decay and death but it's
disguised in theatrical clothes in all its glory and colour; it's fake, but it's death.
When you look at spring, it's promise, new beginnings, another chance, rebirth.
Summer is greedy, ripe, no surprises. With summer it's out there. I like the
winter, the naked trees – at least it's honest.

I'm not good in the wind; I don't mind a breeze but a strong wind makes me
angry. I can go on a bit, my husband says 'Will you shut the fuck up about the
bloody weather', but I really don't like the wind!

The weather most certainly brings me down, more so the older I've got.

I wish it was better. It does make a difference to the character of people.
Nicer weather makes you happier, everything is more bearable.

I love really dark, inky sky but, equally, really sunny is very exciting. The colours are so dramatic. The breeze smells of everything to do with nature. I love bonkers thunder and lightning, and I love the warmth still in the stones at the end of a sunny day.

Where would we be without the weather? I love going into weather conversations. I love watching peoples reactions – 'Oh, bloody hell, is that all she can talk about?' You can tell quite a lot about people's responses when you start conversations about the weather. I'm slightly provocative, if you can't have a good old chin wag about the British weather then you need to climb out of your arse.

I need the sun, I get depressed if I don't see it.

It's the non-weather I don't like.
You get a glimpse of spring then it knocks you right back again.

I like to be warm. I'm enjoying being out in the weather, it's to do with having a dog. I love the weather and embrace it and try to see good in it. If it's a miserable rainy day, it's a 'hot Ribena' day, so it's a lovely day.

I'd quite like it if it only rained at night.

I play a game on my dog walk. When it's grey and miserable I see if I can lift my spirits in my mind to the same feeling I get when it's a bright sunny day. It's a mental exercise, and it works for me.

The 50s

Dress for the weather, embrace the weather.

I love the spring, it's full of promise, and autumn because
it's slightly romantic and sensual.

The minute the sunshine comes out I smile.

It's very important when you've got frizzy hair!
I look at the weather forecast every night.

I'm addicted to looking at the weather, it's the best topic going. I just don't like
the wind though. It's creepy and eerie, it gives me the feeling that someone is
trying to tell me something. It's evil.

Oh, gosh, the weather. When it's hot it's like you're inside a vacuum cleaner.

I check it every day because I'm on playground duty everyday!

I love the extremes. I like being in the Lakes in the pouring rain, heavy gales.
I love the magnitude of weather; crisp cold days with bright sunshine.

I love, love, love the weather. It's a very natural way of connecting with your
senses. I love it when I'm on my bike and the cool breeze blasts my face. You
know, I think it's one of the nicest feelings in the world. I like the rain too. In
fact, I like to stand out in it and get drenched. The seasons are wonderful but
autumn is my favourite. I'm like a child when I see a pile of leaves, I rush
through them and make a mess. Then I feel guilty as the road
sweeper has to do it all again!

The 60s

So, it's happening…If you want to talk to me, don't start with the fucking weather!

I love all weather. I love the absolute pouring rain,
the thunder and lightning, waves …big weather.

I do enjoy the seasons, the changes are interesting. I like it in the winter, curled
up warm and secure. Spring is exciting, blooming and fresh again. Summer you
shed a few things and enjoy it as it is. Autumn, the colours are fabulous,
it's my favourite.

You have to go with what the seasons bring you.
Embrace it all. The seasons are lovely.

The 70s

The sunshine shows the dust!

I love a nice breeze, it washes away the concerns of the day.
I love listening to the birds singing in the garden. I feel free.

The weather can make you feel happy or sad. You wonder about things when
you look up at the sky. I try to read the clouds.

There is someting about the warmth that penetrates my skin and I feel so
protected and comforted.

The 80s

I love the cold. I used to wash my husband's socks and
they would freeze outside on the line.

I have this friend and we both go into a depression on the shortest day. Every
year at the end of this day we phone each other.

I hated the weather when I first came to live here. It was a real culture shock.

The 90s

I don't like it when it's cold. I can't go outside,
and the leaves make it very slippery.

How does it make you feel?

Question 12

What do you think about life – what are we doing here?

As a kid I remember thinking, everything we need is here on the planet. We are equipped for life otherwise we wouldn't be here. I didn't try to understand it, I just knew it had to be right and, if you think about it, everything is here. We have inventive, creative minds and develop all kinds of weird and wonderful stuff and all the ingredients are here. They just have to be formed. That's extraordinary in itself. Something that hasn't even begun its creative gestation is already here. All that is needed is some energy and bingo, it starts to form. Nothing comes from nowhere, friction has to occur, thoughts come, movement happens and that has consequences. From a baby to a piece of artwork, an atomic bomb to an earthquake. I digress…

The responses say it all. You could be sitting around a campfire with a tribe of Native Americans from several hundred years ago and this is the sort of conversation I imagine we would all be having. There is profound common sense and an obvious awareness in every single person's answer.

Over a hundred caring compassionate thoughts can only mean one thing: the womenfolk of this world know what is right and what is wrong. It's all about simplicity, slowing down and using resources efficiently.

Life is a timeline of phases, and the biggest problem of our time is 'no time'. We have become so pressurised, it is almost impossible to live a relaxed pace of life because if you don't conform to the speed then you will get left behind – now there's an idea!

So, imagine you're sat dangling your feet over the edge of the world with your new alien friend from far, far away, she's asking you, 'What's going on down there?' What would you say?

Here are their responses…

The 30s

It's very complicated.

Everyone is trying to find meaning in an unanswerable question!

Life is great, you have to be thankful for being here. There are bad times when I'm fed up, but you have to bounce back. All opportunities – grab them whilst you can. I love living and enjoying life. There's lots to look forward to and sometimes it's the not knowing that's exciting.

Bloody wonderful and bloody hard work. I don't think about it too much or I will have a panic attack. You just have to get on with it.

It's something you have to work hard to fulfil. It's hard work, it's about bonds, friendships, learning to do the best and the right thing as you go along. It's not easy.

Sometimes it's boring and shit and you go, 'Aargh! What's it all about?' It's about learning, and learning about yourself.

Fundamentally, it's about reproducing – we are driven biologically to reproduce. In brief, it's a journey. Did my grandmother think like that? The longer we live the more need there is to create a narrative.

It's a big story book. Everyone is here for a reason with a story to tell.

There must be a point, looking at how everything interacts with everything else, there must be some purpose to it all. I'm so proud of life, particularly nature. Humans try to master it. Mankind and nature manage to rub along quite well.

The 40s

Our role is to remember what we have forgotten, to remember who we really are.

Life changes as you get older. I'm more accepting now. What's the point in pushing to achieve things, for what purpose? We can't effect change any more!

We don't think about the end as much as we should, we don't value it. Life is the most valuable thing in the world and we don't see it like that. I want every minute to count, but life takes over. Don't you think it's amazing when a baby is born, it learns to grow, walk and talk?

There are no winners or losers. It's like a merry-go-round, we can choose to sit on the chicken or the horse but sometimes they're full, so you just have to sit in the car; no-one wants to sit in the car. Have fun, have value. On a micro-scale: keep a family together, mark the holidays, safeguard your nearest and dearest. Eliminate dramas. If you can go macro, change the world!

Life is very basic, it's all very primitive, it's just how it's dressed up.

Don't think about it too much or you'll get into trouble. I approach life quite shallowly, I just enjoy it. Don't worry about the past or the future and don't dwell on the end. My conclusion is that there isn't much more to it, therefore I am determined to enjoy it and have a good time.

Life is exhausting and one day you won't be here and it sends shivers down my spine. Someday you will get to the point when you've had enough. I just want to experience things.

Nature has an awful lot to teach us and we don't pay attention to it.
It's all there for us to see.

You meet certain milestones – but what's the point? I understand why people turn their back on society – it's not a dream, it's a treadmill, pursuing the 'what you're supposed to be doing'. We have invented First World problems. There are people in the world who don't have food; that's real life.

Life is hard, it's a journey of ups and downs, it's a bloody miracle. It's probably too short. It's a blessing. It would be nice to come back again and use what you've learned.

I don't love it all the time, but there are periods when I absolutely love it. I'm glad it's not forever. I feel there are certain experiences that you have to go through.

It's a series of communities trying to live together. It's the essence of humanity. How we relate to each other is really important and how we love and care for each other too. The whole biblical thing, God is on the side of the poor and oppressed, if God's heart is there that's where our own should be. Doing the right thing is important, how you behave: decency, morals and manners.

It's all a bit of a mess. Look at the flowers, plants, grass and go 'Wow, how beautiful and fantastic it is!' Look at nature. It's the nurturing that's gone wrong.

We should care more than we do, people seem to take care of their own and not take care of others. There is no perfect life, we all have to make mistakes and that's OK. We have to learn from our mistakes. People seem to have lost their caring values. When you are born you have a path to lead, you do the best you can with your capabilities. You have choices. Meet every challenge that comes your way. I believe there are tasks we have to face and it's how well you cope with the challenges. It possibly makes you a better person for the next life.

In hunter-gatherer times when people didn't have time to think, they probably didn't care. Now religion has come a long way to make sense of it. Sometimes it's a bit of a chore. Life is nature, it's always there; if there's a God, then nature is it.

You're here for far too little time, make the most of it. It's complicated, we don't make the most of it and I don't understand why, so leave it knowing you've been good and kind. It's pretty monumental.

I'd like to think there is something to it. We come, we go, there's got to be a point or it's pointless? It's what you do with the cards you're dealt. Life is a force that is unknowing, whether it's Buddha or whatever, it's a good way to be.

It's going too quickly. Before I know it I'm going to say, 'What have I done for the last 20 years?' I don't feel much older and, in my mind, I don't get what happened to all that time. Having children: the birth, feeding, a decade goes by – lost. It's a decade of sleep-deprivation, tiredness, it's far too intense. I worried too much and didn't need to.

I want it all to be smiley, nice and gentle. What's the point of life if you don't take pleasure in the lovely things.

Life is a massive lottery. I think life can be amazing and incredibly unfair. You have to strive to be happy in your life, it's not a God-given right.

It's here to be lived. Keep reminding yourself of that, live life to the full. We are not all going to be the best in our fields; Olympians, opera singers and the likes. We don't have to surpass the rest of humanity to have a worthwhile life. Make sure you enjoy and appreciate today and have fun doing it.

Having a purpose, feeling useful, feeling needed and wanted. Having connections with people. It's about having relationships.

It's a state of mind, appreciating what you're doing and what you've got. That's not to say I don't have massive amounts of introspection. You've known yourself all your life, better than anyone else, you've had inner chats with yourself all that time, how can life be lonely?

At worst, something to get through, at best, something to marvel at. The reality of life isn't something that hits me hard. I've taken it for granted. What is the point in it all? When you die, why is it such a big deal? I do find myself saying, 'One day, I will…'

Life is a precious privilege, it's unexpected. I feel my life is incredibly luxurious. Full of choice.

Brilliant! Life is amazing. I enjoy the emotions, even when you're sad. I love the fact that you feel.

What is the point? We all end up as stardust, which can be depressing or inspiring.

Life is for living; enjoying and creating relationships. Finding what you're passionate about so you can do it for work. Learning about yourself, to be responsible for people and the world around you. Finding ways to be inspired by your surroundings.

Boring and dull. Mundanity is actually quite good. Make a difference in whatever it is that you do and bring out the best in people. Join in. If you're on the periphery it's not great.

To be got through, at the moment.

Joyous. To be explored. To look at the sunshine and the rain. Keep on the positive side. It's too easy to slip into sadness and stay there. There is lots to learn, even through pain, there's always a positive outlook, eventually. Keep striving to make the most of what we have been given and keep reaching for more. It's about kindness, giving to one another. Self-responsibility. World peace is about finding peace within. It's a huge, diverse noise. A planet of polarities between light and dark, good and bad. One finds one's peace within the noise. It's a planet of choice and what we choose and how we choose to live doesn't just affect us, it affects everyone.

Life: it's quite scary to think about. It would lead me onto thinking about death. I am much more aware we are on a path and I am pretty far along the path. Life is a positive experience, it's what you make it. Sometimes I have to remind myself of that if I start moaning.

I'd like to believe in reincarnation, but I don't think it's true. I suspect life is a shot we all get, but nobody knows what the hell is going on. We're fumbling our way through. It's a chance to make some magic whilst we are here. You can make some amazing things or create chaos.

Live in the moment. That comes about because of my dad – he's got Alzheimers. Be gracious for what you have. I don't own my own house but I have a roof over my head, I have a nice car, I am grateful for what I've got.

The 50s

It's a few minutes between birth and death.

Life is a hard struggle and unsettling at times. It can be very fulfilling. A learning path, we are constantly learning and teaching everyday. It's a double-edged sword, oppositions and attractions.

We muddle along. I believe we were put here for a purpose, but I haven't found that purpose.

Quite miserable really, there's high points and low points but, the majority of the time, it's quite dull. Sometimes I don't enjoy life, it's repetitive and boring. I like to be busy. I hate being stuck in the house. The world isn't really a nice place, there's too much violence, it's a bit scary.

Life is about renewal, you cannot do life in isolation. You've got to have love in it.

Years ago I volunteered as a prison visitor. I had to fill in a form as to why I wanted to help. My analogy was this: 'Life is like a meadow. There's a gate at each end. We all make our way through the first one and head towards the other. Some will fall in the mud, some will stop and smell the flowers. Why not help and encourage the ones who are struggling? Hold out your hand to the others coming through at the same time as you. Life isn't about how well you do, it's about how well everyone does'.

You breathe in and out. Life is your breath, it's whatever you choose to do.

It's an incredible gift. I believe there is something we don't understand, something unexplained, some kind of energy force.

I think it's about connecting with other human beings. Engaging with this incredible place. You can live life on the surface and really miss the point. There is a mystical, magical wonder to the world. I kind of believe in something bigger than us. When all people come together, there's something powerful that happens.

It's hard, there's no getting away from it, it's not easy. It's also wonderful. I believe in past lives and an afterlife. I do believe in karma, we are here to learn something that maybe we didn't before and that's probably why it's hard.

It's what you make it and how you look at it. Half-full or half-empty.

Society is too negative about life. Today, life is better than it's ever been. Looking at the world from an historical view, we are getting towards a better society and it's nice to be a part of that. To witness people's lives improving. We will get to a Utopian state, just not in our lifetime.

It's a bit of a mess, things have got out of control. It's about power. Power is not always in the right hands. We have the means to feed and house everybody in the world but we don't. I don't know what our overall aim is, our aims have become distorted, we are quite selfish.

I am a bit ambivalent; I want to be a seizer of the day but I am a bit take it or leave it.

If you don't have faith, then there is the lack of an obvious explanation. I don't feel there is an ulterior purpose but I feel, as you've been put here on the earth, so make an effort!

Evolution of the universe. We are part and parcel of something I don't understand. I wonder if there is a reason, is there something missing? It's a bit Groundhog Day. It's going to take time to know how to be, and to be out of the chaos we've created. In a selfish way, it would be nice to be cut off, but then you wouldn't know what's going on in the world.

Everyone is climbing up this imaginary ladder, looking after Number One. People fall down and people don't help. We don't care about one another. When we got to the point of giving children the right to divorce their parents, you create chaos.

Everyone has good in them, it's just dragging it out. There are too many things going on in the world.

My life is about my family and friends. Things I hold dear to me. I'm not a material person, I like nice things but it's not the be all and end all of life.

Because we are all electric, there is energy and if it does nothing more than bring a positive outlook and hope, then so be it.

Life is your breath. You are life. We are life. We are looking outward but it's all going on inward. For example, this morning I opened the back door to let the dogs out and in came the robin, he's our constant visitor.
That's what I love about life.

The 60s

I'm not sure why we are here. Why is it that we have the power and brain capacity to do stuff? Human beings are quite strange. I'd like to think there is a reason. I believe we will become extinct and I hope it happens before the world destroys itself. The day the last man dies then God will die too. God's in your head.

It upsets me that I moan. There are moments when you think you are worse off than others, then you get reminded.

It's a trial by God for the next life; you gotta watch what you're doing.

It's about love, passion, caring and holding. We are part of the natural world, a commune between people.

Life is something you are presented with. You didn't ask to start or finish it, but make the most of it. Be an opportunist. Snatch opportunities when they present themselves. Try and enjoy yourself and do things for other people. Most people I know, once they are retired, do something for others.

It's a joke. It's a beginning and an end. It's a nightmare and a pleasure. It's opposites, fascinating and boring. Life on earth and death on earth. It's opposites, a polarity, a never-ending cycle. Life is a journey, a wonderful experience. It's the attitude you bring to it, it gets better as you get older.

I enjoy life. I've seen a lot of changes. It's who you meet along the way; friends and relatives can have a lot of influence, good and bad. You've got to be upbeat and have friends around you, listen to what they have to say.

What it's all about stems from what I do as a carer for the elderly, what you go through and what is ahead of us.

The 70s

A fucker!

I love life, I don't think a day goes by when I don't say, 'Thank you'. I am so lucky. I still think I'm 21. Life is just a circle, you start as a baby, move round the circle and come back to being that child. I feel a kind of elation.

If we really cared about life we would care about the poor, hungry people. We should respect more. Life is a mystery. Things that we see as important? – it's nonsense. On the one hand we are feeding our pets and, on the other, we eat other animals.

Life is wonderful, but it has its downsides. There are horrendous things happening in the world and you can't put them right. You can make a tiny difference, but not as much as you'd like.

I often wonder what it's all about. I reckon you have to make the most of it. I do think there might be someone there to meet you when you die.

People are very cruel to each other, I can't understand it. Life depends on your birth, it depends on your circumstances, some people's lives must be horrendous. We are lucky to be born in our world, not theirs.

It's a beautiful planet that's sadly spoilt by stupid people. It's magical that we are here.

Life is like a bird pecking at a mountain; it can feel pointless and insignificant and it's easy to feel powerless. I can see we are here to learn and to use our wisdom on a higher plane. There is so much more, I have too many feelings that I can't explain

The 80s

Sometimes life is a pain in the bum. I don't always want to be here. But, saying that, I am very accepting of what life puts in front of me. I don't tend to open up. We are all a little book of stories.

It's a jolly good life. Investigate. Have a good look and make up your opinion.

I am sorry for a lot of people. Things are OK in my little world.
I feel for other people.

I feel very sorry for my grandchildren, I think things are going to be very difficult for them. I'm not big enough to change the world. The police can't even admit they're wrong. People are so devious. Technology is tremendous. Although I can't understand why people go on Twitter and Facebook, I don't understand the point of it.

The 90s

Don't worry about problems that may happen, when they do – deal with it.
Life is to enjoy and be happy.

What does life mean to you?

Question 13

How do you feel about death and dying?

We avoid this topic like the plague. It freaks us out. None of us are deluded about it, we all know it's coming. But culturally it can be tricky to get our heads around.

As a child I used to have an all-consuming fear of dying and it stayed with me until my early 30s. From nowhere this scary feeling would creep up and grab me. It wasn't there all the time but it seemed to get worse the older I got. I decided something had to be done or I felt it would consume me. A friend suggested meditation and it definitely helped. But what really seemed to eradicate the feeling altogether was sitting with mum when she died. Those last moments were as they're supposed to be.

Here are their responses...

The 30s

You have to show your feelings to your children. I'd never seen my Mum crumble. It was only when my grandfather died that I realised she was human. It's important for children to see their parents' emotions.

It's all a bit scary really.

I have a deep fear of leaving my children. It's a common mothering thing. What would they do without me? Death was a deep phobia in my 20s, but now it's OK. Culturally, we are in denial; we think we are immortal and death is handled badly.

I feel afraid of it. Of my own and the death of my loved ones.

Oh gosh, I'm not good at that.

We don't talk about it enough. Most people seem to have a guilt thing attached to death, we don't know what to say!

Dying with dignity, not dying alone; in a peaceful loving environment. I have grown up being afraid of death. Being with people dying has helped.

The 40s

I do believe we go elsewhere, we are in another world.

I was scared of death, but then my granny died and somehow it's given me faith.

If your number's up, it's up! You can't do anything about it. We all die, it's the one certainty. I want the Nolans' 'I'm in the Mood for Dancing'. Then cremate me.

Losing my parents is a toughie.
It's all you've known, now you are the top of the chain.

Life is too short, I am terrified of dying. I am frightened of the idea, I'd love to believe in an afterlife but I don't. One day I will cease to be.

I'm scared of dying, I'd like to live forever.

Life is exhausting, one day you won't be here and it sends shivers down my body.

Death freaks me out.

Unavoidable! It's an individual thing, grief. We think we are unique and indispensable, superior on the planet. We almost think it's beyond us. It's inevitable and I honestly think we are in denial. You don't want to think about it on a daily basis, it's sad.

When I die my monkey mind will be set free and my body will be eaten by worms.

It's pointless to say, 'Why me?' We are all in it.

I don't believe in life after death. Well, I don't know what I believe, actually.
I would like to believe there is a residual essence in you that carries on.
My experience of death has reinforced that when you die, you die.

It's such a hard thing to deal with in our society. People can't express their grief. Society has a problem with mourning. Sometimes people never heal, they are frightened to talk about it.

Death is final, I don't think there is anywhere to go.
Just put me in a cardboard box and carry on.

I don't cope with it. I go to my little house in France (in my head – I don't actually have a house in France!). I cope rather than grieve. I tend not to be as emotional as I should.

Nothing can prepare you for it, but possibly bereavement prepares you for death. I'm not frightened of death.

I do think everyone has a time to arrive and a time to leave.
When it's my time, I won't fight it.

The one good thing about it is that everyone has to go through it. It's the only certainty. Death is final, I don't think there is anywhere to go.

I'm terrified of dying. As a child I would cry myself to sleep.
I am frightened of the idea.

I have been relatively untouched by it until last year. I nearly lost my dad, he had a near-death experience and seeing him in that state was an amazing process.

Take me out of my fucking misery. I've had enough death in my life. I want snowdrops in tin cans and jam jars, and a fucking great big party!

There is no right or wrong way to grieve, you just do what's in your heart. Respect people whilst they are here. The one thing you can't get back is time.

I don't want my dad to die. I don't feel this about my Mum. I feel my dad will go first.

Understanding that everyone has it with them in some way or another. I'm scared of it, as I don't want to die. I'm trying to embrace it, but would rather not think about it too much. I'm scared it will pull me down.

My attitude has changed. I thought death was terrible and crazy and now it just happens, it's inevitable, we all die and I take it a bit more philosophically. You have to keep going, you grieve and there's terrible sadness. My dad died at a similar time that I gave birth. I started to attach positiveness to it. You won't gain anything if you just sit there and think bad of it.

My dad died three years ago. It was amazing – and totally ordinary. It wasn't nice but sadly it was so un-momentous. I wish people had asked me how I was and how I felt, but no one did. I ended up feeling that I couldn't talk to anyone about it.

I see death as a release, going to a higher place. Bereavement is a natural expression of the utter pain of loss of the familiar, a terror of change. Not having the ability to talk or be with the person in the physical, not being able to understand them not being here anymore. It's like a piece of the jigsaw being taken away from you, you are left with a hole you have to fill but don't know how.

I was in Sierra Leone when I got a call from my mum, 'Your grandma is dead'. The response to bereavement in Africa is very vocal, it's not hidden. It's part of their culture and it's very genuine and I got comfort from that.

I was there when my first husband died, and my father. It's very profound when their last breath is taken in front of you.

In a Muslim funeral, everything is very immediate and full of emotion. Nothing is suppressed. We pray, cry, eat, there is so much food. The body is wrapped in a sheet, we all sit on the ground and the face is visible. The body comes very close to you, you can touch it. The body is carried away by the men and they bury it. We wear white not black. There is a real sense that a death has occurred, on a much more guttural level.

There was no message saying, 'I love you' – nothing left.

May 18th 1999 **Back home to find a note – 'David's gone to sleep, forever!' – Shattering!**

My experience of death is that when you die, you die,
and therefore it's more crucial to live the life you want to live.

How lost and alone I feel.

You become untethered.

We don't talk about death enough and as a result you feel unprepared. Death stands side by side with life. Whilst I don't understand it, I do subscribe to things existing beyond life as we know it. I think more people have an awareness of a soul or spirit than they first realise. Our culture doesn't make it easy to talk about death, where others do. I think many more people would be at ease about death if we talked about it more.

I watched my mum take her last breath, it was surreal. If you've never witnessed death before, it's odd. It's completely out of your control, it just happens and the most familiar experience I can relate it to is giving birth. It's like a complete cycle, there's a process, there's stages and in her case it was very intense and took quite a few hours.

The 50s

I feel constrained by sadness.

When my dad died, he was shut out and that hurt me.

I can do this on my own. I'm strong enough. I have made enormous progress, knowing more about myself and my inner psyche is fascinating. It's a source of great comfort. [On grief].

I don't want to think about it. My grandfather said to me 'don't be afraid to die, it doesn't hurt".

We had four deaths last year. It's not fun, but it does change your outlook.

Death is a part of life. It doesn't scare me. My mother can talk on and on about it, she's worried about her funeral, she wants us to go back to her grave, but we probably won't. A grave is a grave.

It just comes along, it's like having a cup of coffee. I don't think anything fazes me anymore; people are here one minute and gone the next.

If anything, it gets harder. When I lost my brother it knocked me for six. I do feel for people when they lose their mum and dad, it's so sad.

You've just got to accept it's coming.

I cried my eyes out when my next door neighbour's dog, Debbie, died. I was seven. I cried more when my own dog died than I did when my mum died. I had a breakdown when my dad died. He died suddenly and unexpectedly. My brother told me off when I suggested Charades around my dad's deathbed. I sang a song on the steps of the altar with my children at dad's funeral. I didn't want to sing with them, but they wouldn't do it alone! It must have been excruciating to watch. When my uncle died, my mum said, 'For goodness sake, take her away, she's making a scene'. As a family, we are uptight at funerals.

I am not qualified to talk about it, I haven't really experienced it. I accept it as part of life.

My mum said, 'I'm dying, I've got to go'. It was a privileged week of our lives. It was a lovely death and it's helped me accept death. The minute she died, a metal door slammed in front of me.

The 60s

It scares me. I can't imagine not being here, not being able to feel again.

I can see how it helps to believe in God, as you get older you probably want to
hedge your bets a bit.

My kids still need me. I'm not ready for death yet, but I'm not frightened of it.

When my husband died, my grief was so much. I just needed hugs,
lots and lots of hugs.

Death makes you grow up. I don't think about it too much.
You can worry about it, but it's not going to stop it from happening.

My dad used to say,
'Put me in a black bag and sling me down the bottom of the garden'.

I stopped having periods the day my husband died. I was 48, it must have been
the shock. When it's my turn cremate me, send me up in a rocket and anything
left scatter it in the Caribbean Sea.

I was encompassed with this grace when my husband died.
I was able to comfort other people.

Your first death is the worst. Once experienced, you're never shy about it. I find
it very easy to talk about it. What I hate most is pretence, what's the point?

You do have to get on with it. If you go backwards you're digging you're own
grave, you have to think about the living.

The 70s

I might cry in private, but I don't want other people to see me.
Maybe I want to be in control.

I picked all the roses from my mum's garden and put them over my dad's body.

I don't want to die but I think, when the time comes, I think you're probably ready. Being a nurse I've laid out a lot of people and I was always scared. I never liked being left in a room alone with a dead body. When you turn a body over, they groan, it's the air coming out of them, it's terrifying. The ward sister would come into the room and open the window to let the spirit out.

I hope it's quick. Both my parents went quickly.
My biggest regret is not being with my mum when she died.

After my mother died, I'd often wish her back, 'Where are you Mummy?' You miss them not being around, for advice. She'd often send me clippings from the newspapers, it's the everyday things you miss.

I'm not keen on going into a nursing home, there has to be a better way. I wish to die in my sleep, it's getting closer and it is on my mind but not all the time. I wonder how I'll cope if my partner goes first.

The 80s

My best friend died at 18. My boyfriend, who I dated from 13 to 21, died in a plane crash. My last words to him were, 'We have our whole lives…' The next thing I heard was his plane came down on exercise in Malta.

It's got to be, so accept it. There's no point being miserable;
there might be a bit of lolly you can spend.

When someone dies, you lose their voice.

Grieving is very important, we weep to comfort ourselves.

The 90s

When I am by myself, I can go into a room and scream.
A hymn will move me to tears. Indians will tell a story, and sing out their grief.

I've planned and paid for my funeral, it's all sorted.

Are you scared of death?

Question 14

What brings you down?

The list is long. There's a lot of stuff that gets to us. I think we forget how sensitive we are. If we did to nature what we inflicted on ourselves, there wouldn't be much left of our world. We are soft sensitive creatures, even the ones with hard shells.

The theme of insecurity and self-doubt is running rife! We've all got 'stuff' and it doesn't seem to matter how much money you have or amazing career you lead, we just seem to be a little bit out of kilter with ourselves.

Here are their responses...

Responsibility

Lack of confidence My behaviour My Mum My own strength Being too hard on myself

My disability Being misunderstood Inability to understand my children Lack of enthusiasm

School demands No support network Falling in love with someone you shouldn't have

Myself Parents Pain Stupidity Hate Arthritis Self doubt The world Loneliness Depression...

My Husband

Trump Melancholy Death Suffering Advantage Money Fear Lack of sleep Control Learning

Health Being upset Rushing Frustrations People Moaning Not saying NO! Chaos Stress

Love Autonomy Money Men Incompetence Entitlement Hormones Lack of choice Illness

Children

Arrogance Weight Anxiety Daily grind Cancer Insecurity Politics

Anger Bad behaviour Holding a grudge Divorce Rowing Housework Lack of Confidence

Tiredness Infertility Old age Rudeness Burdens Lack of connection Ignorance Superiority

Being overwhelmed Negativity Moody kids Injustice Litterers Migraines My brother Politics

Worrying

Homework

Alcohol Dieting Weather Lack of space Indecision Arguments Invasion of privacy My daughter

Bullying Too many people Laziness Bad moods Arguments Invasion of privacy My daughter

ADHD Incontinence My kitchen sink blockage My Mother in-law Stagnation Mundanity

Untidiness Being on my own Criticism Choices The washing Busyness Disappointment...

What brings you down? _____

>> What about Housework?

Repetition of domestic chores get me down and that's why I have a cleaner.

Housework is repetitive and non-productive!

We have defined roles. I do all the cooking, he does the boy's tasks. I don't like him in my kitchen, that's my space.

Housework is bad for the body and soul.

My husband cooks and washes up and I do everything else.

I don't really go in the kitchen or wash up; our roles are reversed.

There are blue tasks and pink tasks. I'm a list person. Give it to the paper.

Chores are dull and boring. Sometimes he'll mop the kitchen floor, but it's very much my department.

I enjoy cleaning when I do it, because it's mindful.

Chores are good for raising children. Housework is utterly compatible with children. The first day of school holidays, I make them do lots of chores then they get out of my sight for the rest of the holidays!

I do like hoovering. I wouldn't like hoovering if it wasn't a Dyson.

I just get the chores done so they don't own you.

I love the clean sheet smell.

December 29th 1997 Washed, washed, washed, ironed, ironed, cleaned!

Cultivate incompetence. If someone thinks you're crap at a job they won't ask you to do it again;

Sylvia Plath had a lovely expression; she considered the household chores the 'mechanics of everyday life'. I like the sense of repeating something every day and getting that calmness, but I also like having a cleaner too.

I'm a cleaner, it's my job. I want appreciation when I'm at work, but I'm not fussed at home.

If you were a Buddhist, you would do your chores mindfully so they wouldn't be like chores. It's to do with living in the moment. If you resent it, you're not living in the moment.

So glad I have a husband to do all that for me.

I do it all; he'll do it if I ask. There's a cathartic element to cleaning; if there's a row about to start, I get stuck into the cleaning. The kitchen sink has to be spotlessly clean. A clean mind equals a clean house.

We aren't very conventional at the husband wife roles; my husband does the shopping and the washing, and Geoff the cleaner does the cleaning.

I only wash the dishes on Sundays.

Chores are a source of contention, I do too much.

I quite like doing things but I usually make an awful mess. I never had to do much. I've always been lucky to pay a char.

He does all the cooking. I've never cooked Christmas dinner in 41 years of marriage.

He loves bleaching the loo.

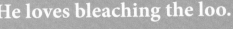

November 7th 1987 Paid the milk bill... £50!

Question 15

What are your views on faith?

W hat is your faith, your philosophy, your spiritual identity? There is so much doom and gloom portrayed by the media that I wanted to know if we still had any kind of faith. Not just religious faith, although I was surprised to see so many different ones amongst these women. Catholics, Quakers, Muslims, Christians, Hindus, Jewish, Rastafarians: the whole gamut. There were the atheists and agnostics too and those whose philosophy on life was about questioning everything. So what is faith? Is it a natural feeling, a tradition, part of our upbringing? Most of these women sang the same song only the language used was different. Does it matter? I don't think so. You know deep down what matters to you and it seems faith is a very personal issue.

Here are their responses...

The 30s

Sometimes it annoys me, everybody is entitled to their beliefs. I don't look down on them for being religious so why do they look down on me?

I pray and I meditate.

The life God put in front of me, if it wasn't meant to be, I wouldn't be where I am. Things always happen for a reason.

Even though there is a spiritual element to my thinking, I don't give much thought to an afterlife. It's important to give your thoughts to this life now, and death is at the end of that.

I believe in fate and the reason why we meet the people we meet in our lives.

To me, being spiritual is trying to understand the people around you, the world and our planet. There is so much more than 'a tree is just a tree'. There is so much more to the world spiritually that people don't see.

The 40s

The notion of death reignites the merry-go-round. I question faith and reincarnation. I don't like to cling to ideas because they are 'nice' or 'suitable'.

I'd like to feel there was something. I say a little prayer, every now and then. I've always prayed since I was a child.

Faith and energy, it does exist but I just can't tap into it.

I don't have much time for religion, it takes away your freedom.

I was brought up a Catholic, just because it's what you do. It kind of angers me now. It's a construct mainly for men to rule over women and people they can bully. It means nothing.

I am a practising Christian, it keeps me going much more than I thought it would. It's about community and spiritual support.

At the end of the day it's religion that is supposed to keep us together but causes more conflict than anything else.

As long as nobody is thrusting it down anyone's throat, I am every man for themselves. I can't be doing with anybody telling someone what to believe in. It doesn't matter what it is; too much enthusiasm pushing something on to somebody is not good.

I am an Ismaili Muslim, I'm not devoutly religious but I like the ritual and I feel at home, connected, in a safe space. It's part of my past. It's an extension of a social life.

If there's a God, I don't want to sit around praying. Religion should be an action not just an idea; not to talk, to do. I am reactive, it's a Quaker thing.

Religion is mad. There's so much fanaticism. I've been brought up a Catholic. I appreciate my kids going to Catholic school, it gives them altruistic values. I like the good things of the Catholic religion, compassion, kindness and then you get into the whole contraception thing: I don't like the hypocrisy.

I wish I had faith but I don't. I'm too rational. The only glimmer was the day I got confirmed. I don't know whether it was God, or me being the centre of attention.

God is what you want it to be, God is anything.
I don't believe in God but I do believe in love.

I do believe in karma and 'you reap what you sow'.

I always go into churches, there's a sense of peace, a sense of stopping, giving your mind a rest, taking a break from the everyday hustle and bustle.

I have prayed with my children although I do have serious questions about the whole Christianity thing. I think the practice of praying, being really honest about things and asking for help is good, as are good morals and reflection. Jesus was all about the underdog.

Always keep your faith, it will get you through.

I thought I used to be spiritual but I am becoming less and less. I'm struggling with the question 'Why are we here?'.

I believe in something, but I'm not religious. There is something and someone looking out for you 'up there' – a guardian angel. White feathers confirm my belief. I don't know what it is, but there's something and it brings me comfort.

I hope I'm learning lessons so next time I come back, I will be nicer.

I don't believe in God, fate is what I believe in.

Spirituality, now that's a whole different ball game. If people deny any spirituality, then they are almost not getting anything out of life.

I believe there is a God, but I have issues with the Catholic faith. I do believe in the afterlife. If you don't ask – and what I mean by that is pray – you'll never know.

I do get funny feelings in our house and catch things out of the corner of my eye. I am open to things.

I'd like to think there is a grand design, but I'm not sure there is. We all search for meaning but find meaning in different things. It's a human impulse.

I think everyone has their own capacity to be spiritual but just don't discover it. I am delighted to be continuously uncovering, revealing and mining my own sense of spirituality.

I pick up white feathers. I have a jar that I've collected. I often see them when I have thoughts or feelings about someone.

The 50s

I have come back to religion, I am C of E. There's a bigger spirit out there, god with a small 'g'. The world has always been driven by wars. I think faith can be a great comforter and a great community binder. I'm not sure how much I believe in the Christian mantra, spirituality gives me peace and space. I find the music very uplifting, socially it's good and I have met some lovely people.

I am a struggling Christian, half on, half off, but I put equal weight on all religions. I envy people with total conviction.

I am a lapsed Catholic and it leaves me cold. I believe in spiritualism, an 'open channel'.

I am an irregular church-goer. It's a jolly happy-clappy church.

Natty dreads, it's a way of life not a religion. You live in a certain way, it's organically grown. I don't do Christmas or birthdays, but when it's my birthday I call it my 'new year'. [On Rastafarianism].

I do pray, it's more of a spiritual thing or putting a thought out there. A lot of Native American stuff resonates with me, the trees, wind, nature interacting. I do believe there has to be more to it.

I need proof to believe. I find it hard to believe in religion, I'm not sure what it gives you!

I don't believe in life after death... well, actually...I don't know what I believe.

I would like to believe there is a residual essence of you that carries on. My experience of death has reinforced that when you die you die!

I believe in fate and the reason why we meet the people we meet in our lives. I believe everything happens for a reason. You have to be quiet to allow those feelings to come. I don't go into my mind so much as you miss out on a lot. If you go searching with your mind you can become tunnelled visioned and forget to acknowledge the tiniest things. I have a friend and we have an inner knowing. We don't need to speak, we communicate somehow without words. It's almost telepathic. There's no superficial chat, it's a shared sense of something inexplicable. I like that.

The 60s

There's someone looking after me and giving me strength.

It can be such a wonderful thing, but so often it's not. It's a source of peace and joy for some people but for others it's the worst possible thing. In the name of religion such atrocities take place and the perpetrator thinks it's OK. Organised religion has a lot to answer for, religious dogma doesn't serve humanity at all.

White feathers are my thing.

I'm a firm believer in prayer, raising your mind and heart to God. Prayer is communication.

I hugely believe in signs and guardian angels.

I like to think there is somewhere people go. Everyone is amazing and incredible, I can't believe there isn't something that doesn't carry on. I want there to be something.

The 70s

I am a half-baked Catholic: it's always best to keep one foot in the door, just in case.

I was at a boarding school where we had to be at Mass every morning at seven. They told us, if you misbehaved you'd go to hell in burning flames of fire. When you're four, that's terrifying.

Before I got married, my godfather said he would play the organ at my wedding. Once he realised I was marrying out of faith, he played at our wedding, closed the lid afterwards and never spoke to me again! If that's religion, you want to take a second look!

I believe there are angels around. There is some kind of force or protection.

I am not religious now because I've had it drummed into me. I can go into a church and feel peaceful but I don't understand religion. It's all gone to pot.

I think it's best just to have blind faith.

When you're dead you're dead, I don't believe in God.

There's something in it but I don't know what.

The 80s

Days before my Mum died she asked me to read her tarot cards.

I like the routine of going to church – if I can't get there,
I join in with the service on the telly.

I believe in God and I have comfort in that.

I saw my doppelgänger in hospital once, she was sat by the
window whilst I was in bed very sick after an operation.

The 90s

There's much more to life than this, it's just beyond our understanding.

Spirituality is how you behave.

I am a Hindu, it's all I know: kind, loving, giving.
It's what I learned from my mother.

Do you have faith?

Question 16

What would you like to leave for the next generation?

Is it the responsibility of previous generations to set the stage for future ones? As modern life changes so rapidly, I was wondering whether our values were changing too quickly too? Will our grandchildren be proud of our legacy?

The responsibility of being an adult, a parent, a teacher and being a role model for the next generation can be a bit overwhelming, but I was comfortably reassured when I asked this question. The answers revealed an overwhelming need to leave something better, something good and something that people will learn from.

Are we supposed to gain wisdom and pass it on? I think so.

Here are their responses...

The 30s

The ability to be content.

Less computers. Less of the crap, let's get back to basics. If you're lost and feeling low, go and make something with your hands.

To even out the balance between the rich and the poor. People to be more equal have more understanding and for there to be way more compassion.

For every child to have food in their mouth. Everybody to have the same amount of money. I wish the divide was more even and we lived in a more harmonious world.

Knowing who you are and not being blown about, not allowing other people to knock you off your course.

To learn a system of apprenticeship, to feel there is a framework to pursue a trade which is well-respected as a professional career. Trades should be as well regarded. I believe we can all be good at something.

For peace, love and harmony and for my spirit to live on. It would be nice for the world to calm down a bit and just get on with life.

The 40s

A bigger sense of community on a basic level, to reignite the community. Be nicer to people and look out for each other.

For a wiser person to come along and help sort out the problems.

Abolition of private schools.

To slow down, taking a step back, looking at the past and taking good stuff from it rather than focusing on the bad. Constant change doesn't necessarily make things better. To look at things ethically.

Focus on things that concern us. Turning down the volume on the vacuousness of the world and turning it up on the valuable stuff, 'proper stuff'.

Self-belief. For kids to be taught they can achieve and how to embrace life.

Nothing! Find it out for themselves. I haven't got any great pearls of wisdom. Make the mistakes, accept the choices that you make. Learn not to regret anything, it's just wasted energy. Make the most of what you've got, there's always somebody worse off.

World peace and compassion for everyone. Will it ever happen?

For everyone to keep learning and reach their full potential. A Steiner approach to health and education, for everyone to learn at their own pace. Where there is no competition. Everyone has good stuff in them, they need to be nurtured by society so that everyone is valued.

Get lost in a book. Don't leave the world full of Kindles and electronic devices. Leave REAL books for our future generations.

I would like to leave a better environment but that's not going to happen. If I could leave my kids the ability to think they can do anything and to go where ever they wanted. That would make me happy.

Open spaces, not concreting over the beauty. To slow down, it's going way too fast. We need to go back a bit, to the old ways. There are too many extremes, too many rich, too many poor.

I'd like to leave choices for my kids. Love thy neighbour as thy self.

For my children to be happy and content with what they've got. To strive to make a difference in the world, for the next generation not to be so greedy. I would like to have the culture of 'being famous for not doing anything' to disappear.

I don't see how this planet can sustain itself and it's going to come to an end at some point.

To be able to provide my children with strength that life is OK and it will be OK. There are bigger things but I want them to see the world as a peaceful place rather than a scary place.

I'm not going to leave my children riches, although there's a few nice paintings that are worth a bob or two! You don't have to be 'Mr and Mrs Breadhead' and crap on people to get through life.

Always forgive and move on. Be an expert on your local area, it's your history. Learn to be capable, help others, work in groups and have leadership qualities.

Genetic screening. Normal is good. Common sense. Stop the quick fixes: we are always trying to solve ourselves socially, physically and emotionally.

A little bit of selfishness is OK, but think about others. And self-belief: this gives you confidence.

We need to work out what we are doing. We are destroying ourselves, killing each other more than ever. I'd like to leave a nice world. Mostly the place is a bit of a mess. Our civilised people need to learn what to do and divide the riches a bit better. There's so much and there's so little.

Always try to be positive: where there's a will, there's a way. Even though I don't act on that myself. If you have a goal, try to achieve it.

I would like to leave a confident woman behind who is sure of herself and not overly-influenced by my fucked-up relationship with her father.

Peace, calm, self-knowledge, true honesty – and lots and lots of trees.

I do hope the world doesn't explode. I hope there is a world for the future generations. I would like to leave a legacy of love, warmth, respect for others and for my children to say, 'Oh yes, my mother was the best mother you could ever have'.

For children to believe in themselves but not to be selfish and that, I believe, equals confidence.

My artwork. Hope and awareness. Our future is our responsibility. Be confident with the voice you have and speak out for injustice and truth. Confidence is more important than ego.

Have an impact on people in a positive way. Be yourself. Take a chance and live whilst you're here. It's easy to go through life going through the motions and not following your heart and not getting from life what you want. People are all fighting demons. What looks different on the outside, isn't necessarily what's on the inside.

The 50s

I hope I'm not screwing my kids up. The most important thing is for my kids not to think of me as my Mum did of me. I'd like to leave happy memories, happy kids, that can add to society rather than take away. I think very few people leave a mark.

I don't like to see kids suffering, no-one should be starving or homeless in this day and age.

Insight to human traits, a better understanding that we are all meant
to be different. Acceptance, tolerance and good manners.

For my family to have a knowing connection with themselves and to know that
nothing is that important.

There's no respect for the elderly. Old people are wise and they have something
to teach us, they know stuff we can't understand. We should be forgiving and
understanding.

Take responsibility for yourself, respect for others and yourself.
To live every moment that you possibly can, with grace and joy.

To leave a positive attitude. When you feel down about things,
think about the bigger picture, and pass that attitude on.

To instil good values in my children. Why can't people learn to live together;
why is there so much intolerance?

I have already left a pedestrian crossing that I campaigned long and hard for!

Lots of advice as to what's gone on in the past in order to make future lives better.

More trust and appreciation of the simple things in life,
get rid of some of the extremes.

The 60s

I'd like to leave a fab piece of architecture, the love of nature and the appreciation
of beautiful things. I hope someone stops London becoming like New York – so
many of our beautiful buildings are being replaced by glass.

We need reminders of what has been in order to prevent it happening again.

For people to have insight into each other, to be uncritical
and have mutual understanding.

If you have a skill, leave traces of yourself behind.

Leave everybody knowing that they are never alone, there is unseen help that
they can call upon. To leave them knowing we are all connected. All we really
want to be is to be loved and peaceful.

I wish the political situation was better and then there wouldn't be so much
unrest in the world.

The Earth is giving life, treat it with respect,
help to keep the planet good for the next generation.

The 70s

Harmony: I have worked all my life to keep everybody in harmony.

I'd like to leave the world a better place than when I came into it. To live in a
joyous, happy country, without any greed or aggression. For people to be
helping, kind, thoughtful and loving. As you get older you realise the world isn't
the place you thought it was. The things you took for granted when you were
younger are very valuable.

My generation has had the best years, there doesn't appear to be a lot going for
the world at the moment. It's a sad world with bitter people,
I hope it doesn't get any worse.

Not to have any of these horrible world issues that are going on.
I hope my grandchildren remember me.

The 80s

Enough food for the world, more common sense. Peace and stability.

Think very hard about family life, it's a big commitment.
Don't do too much and have a sense of responsibility.

Good health; you can cope if you're healthy but if you are in a
state of collapse, it's not good.

The 90s

Try a piece of humble pie every now and then; it can be quite nutritious.

To love each other, be more tolerant and spread more joy.

What would you like to leave?

Question 17

How do you best express yourself?

When I asked this question I'd occasionally get a blank look as if to say, 'I speak!' But it was more than just talking. It was those less obvious expressions; the ones that have been part of our psyche for so long that we take for granted. Pondering this question was fascinating.

Maybe it was that she always wore red lipstick and re-applied after every meal? Or the way she dressed with such simple elegance that she almost appeared ethereal? Or in the confines of her car she belts out Elvis. I love this question, it really makes you think about what you do and how you do it. It gives you a renewed appreciation for YOU!

Here are their responses...

Singing in the car

Photography Gardening Thinking Singing Verbally Gesticulating Screaming Being tactile Sewing Touching Hair Dancing Art My job Relationships Flowers Shouting Aesthetics ...

Singing

...Music Movement Letter writing Clothes Cooking Rushing Words Ballet My opinion

Reading Writing Swearing Colour Laughing Facial expressions Gurning I'm thrifty

Giggling Crying Writing diaries Acting Through my actions Whistling De-cluttering

Wearing black Twisting my hair Ranting Drama Collecting things Pulling silly faces

Hoarding Cackling Nagging OCD I'm a neat freak Nurturing Silence Lipstick Language

Controlling Taking over the Karaoke Talking to myself Knitting Line dancing High heels

Dying my hair different colours Hair Calligraphy By my hospitality Through Make up...

Singing in the shower

How do you express yourself... _____

>> What Concerns us?

My biggest regret is not having achieved whatever it is that I am supposed to have achieved.

He suppressed me more than I realised.

Fear stops you enjoying things

I was an auxiliary nurse. I didn't want to climb the career ladder, I wanted to be at home with the kids. My husband said I was 'just a maid'.

Bullying stripped away a lot of my confidence. I was so diminished by seven years of it that it made me look for security in relationships.
I was looking for security instead of trying new things.

I don't think I'm bright enough.

I wrote a poem and my teacher accused me of copying it as he couldn't believe I'd written it.

Both my parents were unreliable.

When I first starting teaching in the Seventies it was wonderful, your own love and enthusiasm rubbed off on the kids. When I came back to it in the Nineties, it was totally different, box-ticking, soul-destroying, crowd control. I didn't sign up to be a social worker.

My parents dissuaded me from becoming a doctor, 'We don't think you are symapthetic enough'. Then later in life they said 'We thought you'd have made an excellent doctor'.

We encourage our kids, but nobody encouraged me.

My Mum said 'you're past your best'. I was 35!

My Mum hated the fact I was so independent. She wanted me to be reliant on her and I wasn't.

24th May 1994 **Repossession date through!!!!**

My Mum was facially scarred by acid in a chemical explosion when she was 21. She never looked pretty. I'd always been bothered by it, then one day talking with one of her old friends, I found out her scarring had never bothered her. In fact what I'd been doing was carrying around my own issues and angst about it.

Dumping me in a boarding school was worse than dumping me on the street.

Fear stops you trying new things.

Rigidity equals a closed mind.

My Mum made me doubt myself the whole time. I loved her and we got on great, but I felt I could never do right.

My music teacher rapped my knuckles and, consequently, I stopped playing the piano.

Being groped by my driving instructor was creepy. I was 17 years old and these ageing hands slid round the back of my back whilst I was in deep concentration then, lo and behold there they were on my boobs!

What you never gave me, mum, was time. You were always working, you never came to watch.

I can't abide women looking like they're on their last legs, struggling, pained walking, straining to get up from the table.

I usually keep my opinion to myself as it's not usually valid.

I strive for my Mum to tell me she loves me, without having to prompt her.

The things some people have said to me whilst working as a traffic warden, 'I hope your kids get cancer and die' or, 'I hope you get run over by a bus'.

She's like a flower that's blossomed. Overblown and gone blowsy, with dead bits on the end. She's past her sell-by date. There's a moment when they've been in the house too long and they start to smell. *[A daughter about her mother].*

I wanted to be a hairdresser. I thought it would be glamorous, but my mum wouldn't let me.

14th July 2004 Feeling one degree under — must sort out cancer pills

Question 18

What have you taken from today?

Now it was my turn to squirm. This question hadn't been on my original list until Jheni piped up, 'You need feedback; you need to know what people think about doing something like this. What have they got from it? You know, reflection'. I was to ask what they thought about my whole project, and I'm glad I did. Reading the comments really does tell you that we need to take time out for each other.

Here are their responses...

The 30s

It's nice to stop and talk like this, it helps clarify things. You don't often stop and think. I'm always indulging, judging, being harsh on myself. I felt it was quite self-indulgent, but actually a good thing.

Quite self-indulgent talking about me. I enjoyed the exercise, soul-searching. It was quite therapeutic, thinking a lot about myself for once. I learnt a lot about me, like that I am OCD!

I do like certain things about myself and it's highlighted that I have moved on a lot since January when I was in a state. I feel more content.

Your first answer can lead onto something else, the digression leads to another issue that you wouldn't have necessarily linked together. I was quite nervous when we first sat down because of the fear of exposing myself. I'm not very forthright with my opinions.

It's been brilliant! I can't believe what I've told you, it's not what I thought it would be. It's good to reflect on stuff. It's made me feel good about myself, focused me in on what I really want.

I have realised that I don't have to try so hard. I can stop thinking about trying to achieve the next thing. I am much happier about living in the moment.

I can relate to you and it made me feel very comfortable.

The 40s

Very uncomfortable. I have learnt that I have more work to do on accepting myself for who I am.

It made me realise that we are similar in the way we think and feel. It's like I am talking for lots of other people, too. It's made me address issues that might not have been addressed otherwise.

It's a good thing to do. I can't say I was looking forward to it. It was a bit daunting.

Sitting and thinking about myself. Focusing on things I need to address.

I am quite a simple person. I don't suppress my feelings. I'm not hiding behind anything, what you see is what you get. I'm not suppressing life.

It was liberating and refreshing to discuss me. A couple of issues have come out that I don't think I would have said out loud. There's stuff I wouldn't have realised about myself.

I have sore cheeks from laughing! I realise I am more positive than I thought I was. It was a very enjoyable, funny experience.

Time to talk, share, listen and not feel bad or silly. I want to work on my confidence and self-esteem.

It's been quite an intense day, you've made me explore things I've been avoiding. I know I need therapy in some way. It's been uncomfortable admitting that I'm not a nice person sometimes. You've seen the vulnerable side of me. I realised that, spending the day with you, I have been ignoring my spiritual side. Maybe that's what I've been missing.

September 8th 1996 Verona with Cyn for my 50th, kindly man held my hand for lift off

Taking someone out of their comfort zone and pushing the boundaries.

It's been rather lovely. A timely thing, at a state of change in my life. It's been nice to spend time thinking about stuff.

I've realised I've been plodding along and it's not alright.

It re-asserts who you are. It's made me think about taking risks and wanting a challenge. Maybe deep sea diving in Egypt next year!

You can do something about your flaws!

Thinking and reflecting on my life and how things have changed since my 30s. Suddenly everything has fallen into place. It was so chaotic and wrong before, now I am seeing the benefits of my hard work.

A thoughtful and provocative experience, but not demanding. It was easier than I thought it was going to be, it coincided with life-changing things too. It's made me think. The last 18 months for me, have been quite challenging.

I've seen my friend that I haven't seen for a long time. It's better than a session with a counsellor. It's really weird that I haven't been able to talk about my situation but I felt, here, that I've worked through a few things and feel clearer.

I found the questions difficult to answer. You'd think they would be simple, but they're not. I think it's been difficult but very cleansing and good fun. I've enjoyed it.

I need to be a bit more adventurous, get out more and do stuff: travelling, photography – and I need to lighten up on my daughter.

How very easy it is to talk to you. It's very thought-provoking thinking about the questions. I did get very upset when I said I had no dreams, I don't want to end up closed off. I need to be careful, I don't want to end up with no enthusiasm. Be involved in the world. It made me think about things, it's a good thing. You can't live your life with your head in the sand, that equals fear! Those are the things you regret on your deathbed.

To be kinder to myself, more relaxed and forgiving of myself. To give myself a break. It's been quite healing, talking. I've realised that selfishness isn't really selfish. I'm very honest with myself. I know what I should change. It was calming and soothing. I feel I have tidied everything up.
Now I need to act upon things.

It's a bit like therapy, 'me' time, guilt-free time.
I have found myself thinking, 'What are my highlights?'

It's taught me to dig a bit deeper. Why don't I like help? How can I be comfortable having nice things? Instead of giving it out, take it in.

It's the best time you'll spend, precious, valuable. Thank God for this time, there's something angelic, healing and caring about this process.

The 50s

I have learnt that I am a bit down on myself.

I am normally more restrained and I'm surprised I've let out as much personal stuff as I have. I'm happy hearing that other people go through similar things and I hope it kicks my butt into gear. I do want to change the broken record!

We all need love, recognition and stability.
All requirements for the human condition.

March 26th 1998 **Car parking ticket!**

It's been very therapeutic, it's not often you get a chance to talk about yourself without feeling self-conscious. I love talking about myself. Even the worst things talked about are less scary. It's good to be honest and open about oneself, I'm very rarely truly honest.

I am going to go away from this far more positive. I feel very inspired. I am going to get my arse in gear and 'do it'!

I have realised that my daughter will make her own choices in life and I should try not to control as much as I do. I felt I was judging her, but realise now that I just wanted to protect her. I want to make her future bright but I can't control that, it's her destiny.

It's a privilege to be asked to reflect on my life in good company.

I am glad I did it. I found I cried a lot, which was a release. I cry at everything; I didn't realise I saw the world that badly. It's just how I feel at the moment.

It's confirmed that I am on a path of improvement. A better person than I was ten years ago. I'm much more sorted, much happier and nicer to live with. I am bloody lucky and fortunate and it's really important to give some of that back.

I am going to look at my garden in a new light, and stop running away. I have a self-destruct mode. I avoid things by going out, I'm running away from my haven and myself.

Doing this has brought back some good memories. Telling someone about where you come from is living the memory; I can actually see St Lucia whilst we are talking about it. Walking someone through my history. We always have to remember where we come from.

It's a good thing to do, offload your jibber-jabber. It's interesting to look at your character traits. It's good to think about things and express them. Sometimes it's not easy to put into words what's going on.

I didn't realise that life inspires me, but it does. I like life, it's important to know what you need. If you can get to middle age and know what you need and how to get it, then that makes me a happy bunny.

The 60s

It's an enormous privilege to sit and talk confidently about what one thinks about in one's life.

I didn't know what to expect, some of the questions are quite difficult. To look at yourself, it's quite a good thing in a way. I look forward to spending more time on myself. More time for friends, going out shopping, have a bite to eat, making new friends.

I've enjoyed it, it's unearthed my emotions – it's raw – but that's OK.

Time spent like this brings back clarity on what you already know.

People feel guilty about taking time out for themselves these days, but we shouldn't!

The 70s

Perhaps I should be more aware of my judgemental nature.

Talking and telling is an interesting journey. It's like I'm hearing myself clearly.

Maybe you have to better yourself all the time throughout life. I think you've got to be capable of changing your opinion, not to have tunnelled vision. Be flexible and be a good listener.

The doing is more important than the achievement.

Today has been rewarding and stimulating.

The 80s

I think we're all a little book. We all have a story to tell.

Very inspiring! Thank you for giving me much to think about.

Have you enjoyed your time?

Conclusion

Having these conversations has magnified how important it is to talk. Conversations are much more than dialogue. Often it's the unsaid, the space around the words that says so much more and that's what's missing when you're texting, emailing, or even chatting on the phone. You have to be actually there, present. It's a connection that goes much deeper. Having listened to all these women, I know quality conversations are needed more than ever.

Over the four years collecting conversations, I can safely say I understand what's going on inside the hearts and minds of today's women. I know this isn't an anthropological study but I think I can conclude that we are surprisingly very similar and perhaps much more so than many of us might think.

Yes, some of us may be able to shout louder, express ourselves more clearly, ooze confidence or give the impression of a 'coper' and perhaps this is what you were looking for whilst reading this book. By comparing ourselves, seeing if we are doing life the 'right' way? After all, we don't come into the world with an instruction manual. Perhaps it's by comparing that we can understand who we are a bit better and either accept ourselves or see possibilities for change; one thing's for sure, we are fascinated by how other people experience life and we want a little honest insight.

Patterns emerged; worries and self doubt flooded every conversation as did wise words, sensitivity and kindness. We'd veer 'off' topic, deviating from the serious to the trivial in mid sentence.

The contradictions came in by the bucket load. For instance, when I asked one woman how she was, she said, 'I'm happy and content, life is good', followed in the next breath by, 'I'm so fat, I hate myself!'

Confidence and body image issues were off the scale. But equally when I asked about 'bigger issues' like our thoughts on life, children, and our responsibility for the world, I didn't hear anything that reflected low self-esteem and self-doubt; quite the contrary.

Loneliness echoed throughout. Hearing this made me realise how quick we are to cover up the way we feel with quick fixes; shopping, drinking, social

media etc. There was an audible sigh of relief when I could offer genuine reassurance that as uncomfortable as these feelings are, they are 'normal' and we aren't as alone as we think we are.

There was enough passion and enthusiasm to change the world over and many lightbulb moments of clarity. Some days we can set the world on fire and on others, we want to give up and crumble but, for most; it's just Ground Hog day.

If I had to try and summarise what I'd learned it would be:

- Being stuck isn't a permanent state, change is always around the corner.
- It's not easy but we do have a choice to change the way we think.
- Change what isn't working, even if it takes time.
- We expect way too much of ourselves and others.
- Spending time by yourself and getting to know who you are is probably the best advice.
- There is something so simple and comfortable about sitting down at the kitchen table and sharing.
- And my favourite: **Never assume anything about anyone, ever!**

After reflecting on what I heard, inevitably I had more questions:

- Why do we constantly put ourselves down, and I don't mean humorous self-deprecation?
- Why can't we see that worrying is pointless?
- What would happen if we recorded a conversation and heard it back? Would we notice our inconsistencies and contradictions?
- Why do we expect so much from ourselves and others?
- What or who is it that we are trying to control?

I don't have the answers to these questions but perhaps having a little more understanding of ourselves is enough!

The End

I'm happily exhausted and it's time to stop typing and wish you well on your journey through life. Before I go, please remember that our worries and self doubt aren't going away anytime soon. I'm afraid they seem to be part of our make up, but I hope that having read what you've read, you'll spend less time worrying. And with all that extra time you've created, why not ask a friend round, stick the kettle on and start a conversation. Illuminations are nearer than you think.

I'll leave you with these two quotes I found:

Eckhart Tolle author of 'The Power of Now' said –
'Worry pretends to be necessary but serves no useful purpose at all'.

And from the tv series 'Last Tango in Halifax': written by Sally Wainwright –
'Life is about confidence. The only way to get confident is to put yourself into situations you feel are out of your depth. When you feel uncomfortable and have been around people you don't feel comfortable with, then you become confident' – she's not wrong!

Thank you for reading. Thank you for listening.

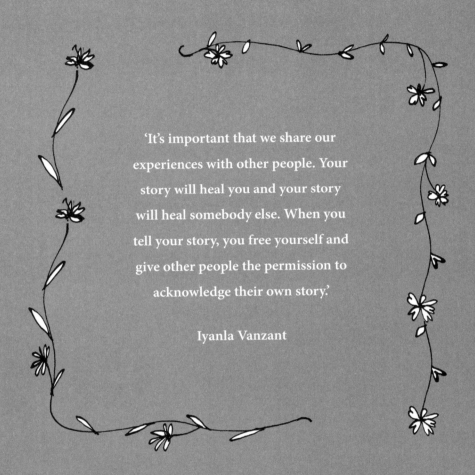

'It's important that we share our experiences with other people. Your story will heal you and your story will heal somebody else. When you tell your story, you free yourself and give other people the permission to acknowledge their own story.'

Iyanla Vanzant

Notes

....

....

....

....

....

....

....

....

....

....

....

....

....

....

....

Notes

Notes

....
....
....
....
....
....
....
....
....
....
....
....
....
....
....
....

Notes

....
....
....
....
....
....
....
....
....
....
....
....
....
....
....
....

Books that have helped me along the way…

May I recommend these books. They correlate to the themes in my book: death, grief and loss, self-help, women, memoir, inspiration, and social and oral history.

They're a selection that have helped me; some for research, others simply inspired me. But, as any good book should, they have opened me up and made me curious.

Death, grief, loss

Frankle, Viktor, E. 'Man's Search For Meaning', Rider, 2004.

Lewis, C.S. 'A Grief Observed', Faber & Faber, 1961.

Porter, Max, 'Grief is the Thing with Feathers', Faber & Faber, 2015.

McElhone, Natascha, 'After You', Viking, 2010.

Strayed, Cheryl, 'Wild', Atlantic books, 2012.

Albom, Mitch, 'Tuesdays with Morrie', Bantam Doubleday Dell Publishing Group, 1999.

de Hennezel, Marie, 'Intimate Death: How the Dying Teach Us How to Live', Alfred a Knopf, 1997.

Kubler Ross, Elizabeth, 'On Death & Dying', Prentice Hall, 1997.

Self-help

Whyte, David, 'The Three Marriages', Penguin, 2009.

Levoy, Greg, 'Callings', Harmony Books, 1997.

Winfrey, Oprah, 'What I know for Sure', Macmillan, 2014.

Ramen, Rachel, 'Kitchen Table Wisdom', Berkley Publishing Group, 1996.

Grosz, Stephen, 'The UnExamined Life', Chatto & Windus, 2013.

Roosevelt, Eleanor, 'You Learn By Living', Hutchinson, 1961.

Tolle, Eckhart, 'The Power of Now', New World Library, 2010.

Greenhalgh, Wendy Ann, 'Mindfulness & the Art of Drawing: The Creative Path to Awareness', Leaping Hare Press, 2015.

O'Donohue, John 'Anam Cara', Bantum Press, 1997.

Women

Sharan, Farida, 'Creative Menopause', Wisdome Press, 1994.

Northrup, Christiane, 'Women's Wisdom Women's Bodies', Judy Piatkus, 1995.

Northrup, Christiane, 'The Wisdom of the Menopause', Random House, 2012.

Murray, Jenny, 'The Women's Hour', BBC, 1996.

Inspirational & research

Rebanks, James, 'The Shepherd's Life', Penguin, 2016.

Neill, Robert, 'Mist Over Pendle', Arrow Books, 1971.

Winterson, Jeanette, 'Why Be Happy When You Could Be Normal?',
    Vintage, 2012.

Aurelius, Marcus, 'Meditations', Penguin Classics, 2006.

Beatty, Melody, 'Journey to the Heart', Harper One, 2010.

de Botton, Alain, 'The Course of Love', Hamish Hamilton, 2016.

Pepys, Samuel, 'Diaries', Penguin Classics, 2003

Lewis- Stemple, John, 'The Running Hare: The Secret Life of Farmland'.
    Doubleday, 2016.

Jeffers, Susan, 'Feel the Fear and do it Anyway', Rider, 1997.

Fraser, Henry, 'The Big Little Things', Seven Dials, 2017

Jung, Carl, 'Mémoires Dreams & Reflections', Fontana Press, 1995.

Oral & social history

Bronson, Po, 'What Shall l Do With My Life', Vintage, 2004.

Stanton, Brandon, 'Humans of New York', Macmillan, 2015.

Johnson, Tracy, 'The Mill Girls', Ebury Press, 2014.

Taylor, Craig, 'Londoners', Granta Publications Ltd, 2012.

Usher, Shaun, 'Letters of Note', Canongate, 2013.

Burns Catherine, 'The Moth' Serpent's Tail, 2015.

Hanauer, Cathi, 'The Bitch is Back', William Morrow, 2016.

Bennett, Alan, 'Untold Stories', Faber & Faber, 2006.

Acknowledgments

Whenever I've read acknowledgments in books I've never understood why there are always endless lists; now I do. It's true, and a cliché, but there's no way this would have got past the first year without all these people to help, inspire and encourage me. I am very grateful first and foremost to Jheni, without whose enthusiasm I would have never taken up this challenge.

I would like to thank all 107 wonderful women for allowing me access to their inner thoughts.

To Gastro coffee house in Clapham, where it all began. To Carrie, for defining structure. Judy, the O'Tooles, Emma B, Maggie, Teresa, Caroline E, Clare T, Jane, Shelley, Lynn, Jackie W and Teri, for being kind enough to read earlier versions which enabled me to keep learning from my mistakes. To Saffron, Irene, Helena, Polly and Trev for explaining to me in simple terms what I needed to do. To Clare M for giving me extremely honest feedback in my last version, and trying to guide me in the right direction. To Aysha and Mark, my Beta readers. To Ross, for a sharp word in my ear at a time when I really had had enough. For my friends on Facebook, because when you work by yourself at home all day, it gets very dull. And to Jayne who after meeting on a train a few years ago agreed to write the forward.

Thanks to Su, my editor… what can I say? You're a patient woman! And to Sian who painstakingly proof read.

To Charlotte for her gorgeous illustrations and Alison for taking my Blue Peter style, sticky mess and making this book beautiful.

To my family; Sally, Carole, David and Amanda for endless positivity and encouragement, to Elaine, my oldest friend, for having always been there and June my wisest counsel; James, my son, for constantly asking 'When's it finished? To my girls, Connie and Anna, for periodically reading Mum's diary entries out aloud, a lovely reminder of times gone before, and lastly to Martin, my husband, who kindly puts up with me.

A final word of thanks to Mum. She was a kind, straight-talking, down-to-earth woman who always said what she thought. She is missed.

THANK YOU